Silver and Glass

Cornelia Parker and Photography

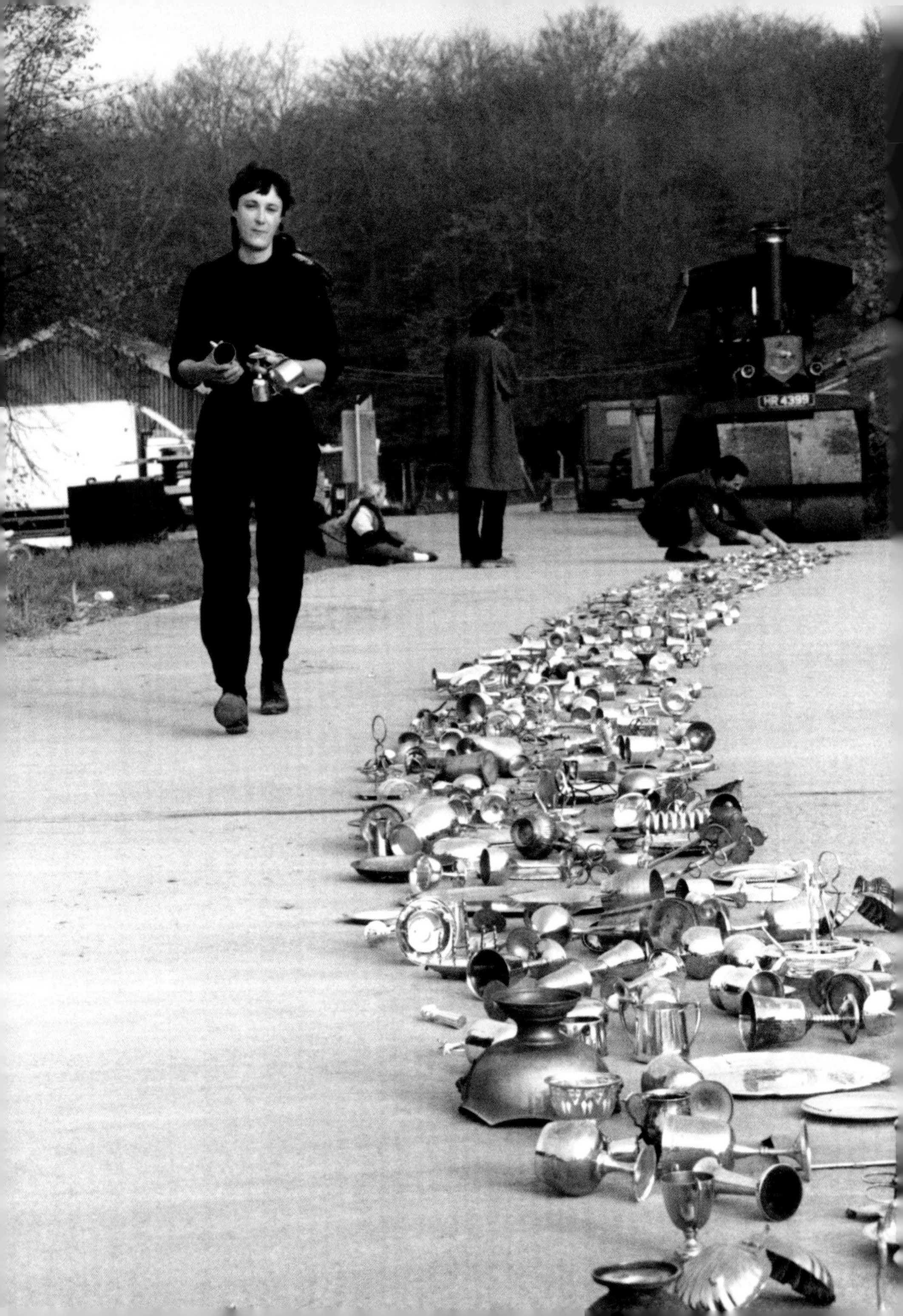

Silver and Glass
Cornelia Parker and Photography

With contributions from
David Campany, Cornelia Parker
and Antonia Shaw

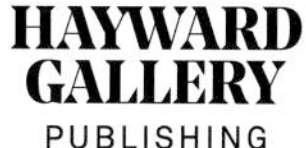

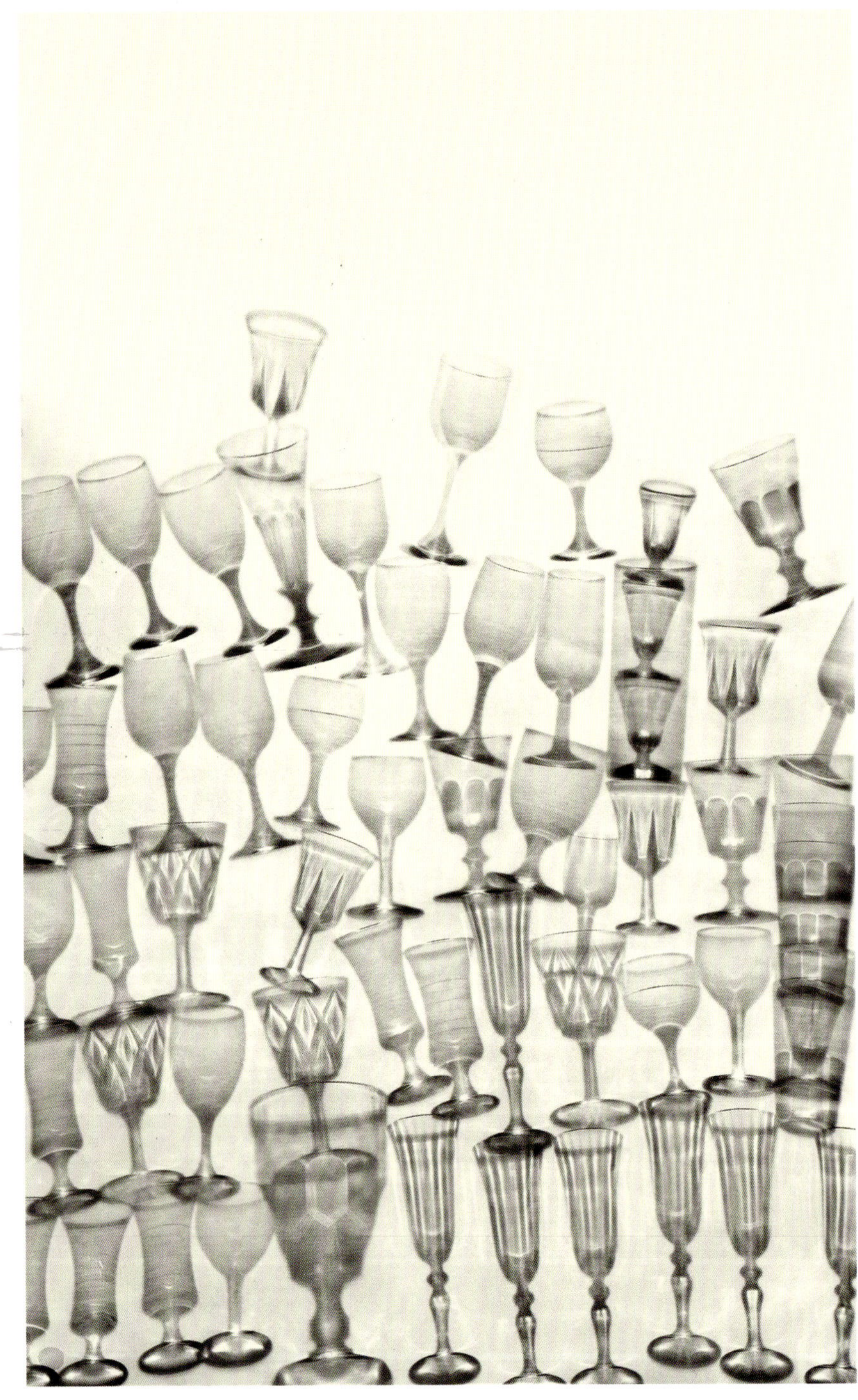

Contents

Foreword

It seems natural that an artist as inventive and inquisitive as Cornelia Parker should be fascinated by the mysterious alchemical processes of photography, especially as these were first made manifest in the medium's early experimental years. This, combined with a propensity for collecting the residual traces of historical figures and reinvesting them in the here and now, makes her recent series of prints derived from the silverware and glassware of the photographic pioneer William Henry Fox Talbot a perfectly logical fulfilment of a lifelong obsession. The translation of three-dimensional objects into two dimensions, whether by literally flattening them with a steamroller or creating a ghostly impression on paper as in the photogravures reproduced here, is a consistent trope in Cornelia Parker's work dating back to her seminal sculpture *Thirty Pieces of Silver*, produced, as it happens, 30 years ago at time of writing.

The prints in her recent series, *One Day This Glass Will Break*, *Fox Talbot's Articles of Glass* and *Thirty Pieces of Silver (Exposed)*, are no less revolutionary and haunting. It was while thinking about a publication to accompany the Hayward Gallery Touring exhibition *One Day This Glass Will Break* – consisting of a selection from all three series – that we decided to extend the discussion beyond those particular prints to a wider consideration of the artist's relationship to the conceptual and technical implications of photography in her practice as a whole. In her essay, Antonia Shaw, the curator responsible for the exhibition, considers William Henry Fox Talbot's influence on Cornelia Parker's photogravure prints. The conversation that follows between the artist and photography critic and curator David Campany explores how notions of photography have infiltrated and informed her practice. Taken together with illustrations from across her career, these texts reveal how the medium continues to orbit in what Campany calls Cornelia Parker's 'artistic universe'.

For their invaluable contributions to the making of this book and the exhibition that inspired it, I join Cornelia in thanking Antonia Shaw of Hayward Gallery Touring and Rebecca Fortey of Hayward Gallery Publishing, Cornelia's studio manager Caroline Smith, graphic designers Herman Lelie and Stefania Bonelli, and Alan Cristea and Luke Duncan of Alan Cristea Gallery.

Roger Malbert,
Former Head of Hayward Gallery Touring

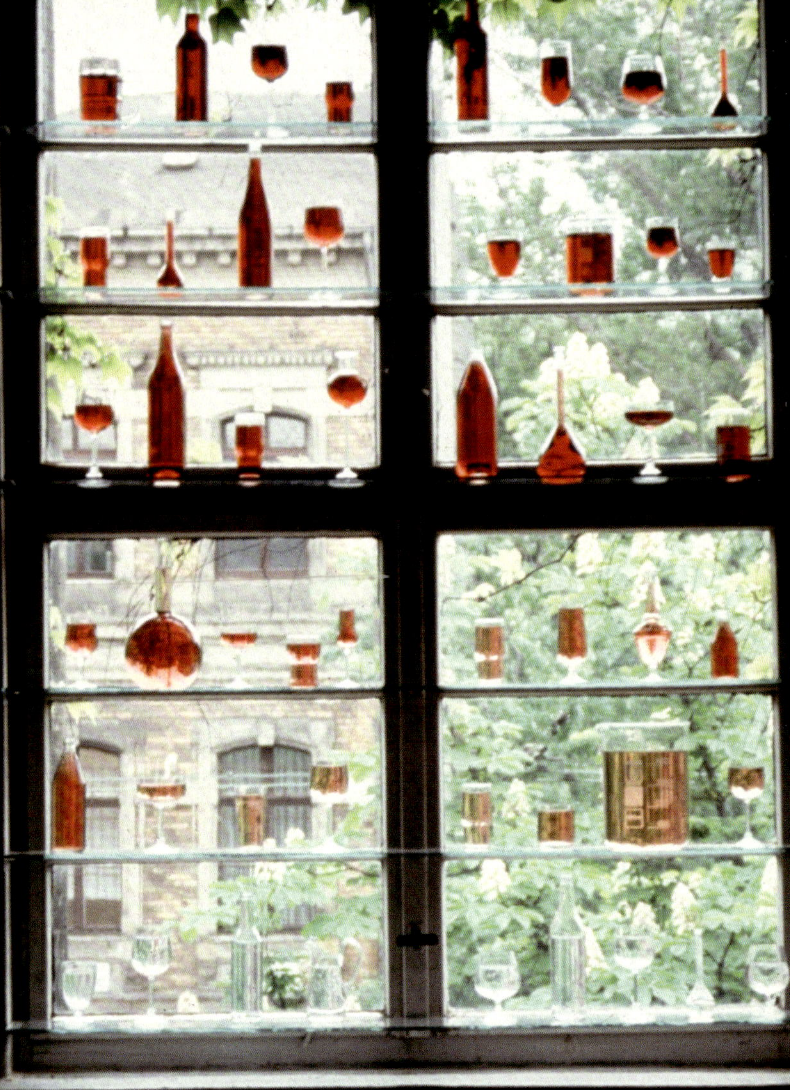

One Day This Glass Will Break

Antonia Shaw

> *The changing of bodies into light, and light into bodies, is very comfortable to the course of Nature, which seems delighted with transmutations.*
>
> Isaac Newton, *Optiks or a Treatise on the Reflexions, Refractions, Inflexions and Colours of Light* (1704)

If we can see a world in a grain of sand, then maybe we can imagine the merging of many worlds when we look at glass – made, as it is, from melting the stuff. When subjected to extreme heat the raw mineral transforms into a molten liquid before solidifying into a transparent mass. An industrially produced pane of glass can be almost imperceptible to the eye. If we are not careful we can walk slap-bang into it, because we don't see glass exactly, we see *through* it to the world beyond; we see its frames and shadowy edges, and the effects of its transmission of light. We see *with* glass too. Lenses in spectacles and telescopes aid our vision and fill the apertures of optical devices. When we perceive glass we are actually seeing interferences with it, ruptures and reflections or the distortions it creates. Concave or convex glass warps the forms that sit behind it. Cracks and scratches, dirt and ripples draw our attention to its surface, and light bounces off it, creating flashes of luminosity and mirror images.

We primarily think of glass as a man-made product, but it also occurs naturally. Glowing magma produces black volcanic glass when it spews over sandy sediment, and if sand is struck by lightning it fuses together and vitrifies into hollow, tubular quartz known as

Another Matter 1993
Water, wine, glass vessels and glass shelves, dimensions variable
Installation in 20 windows, Grassimuseum, Leipzig

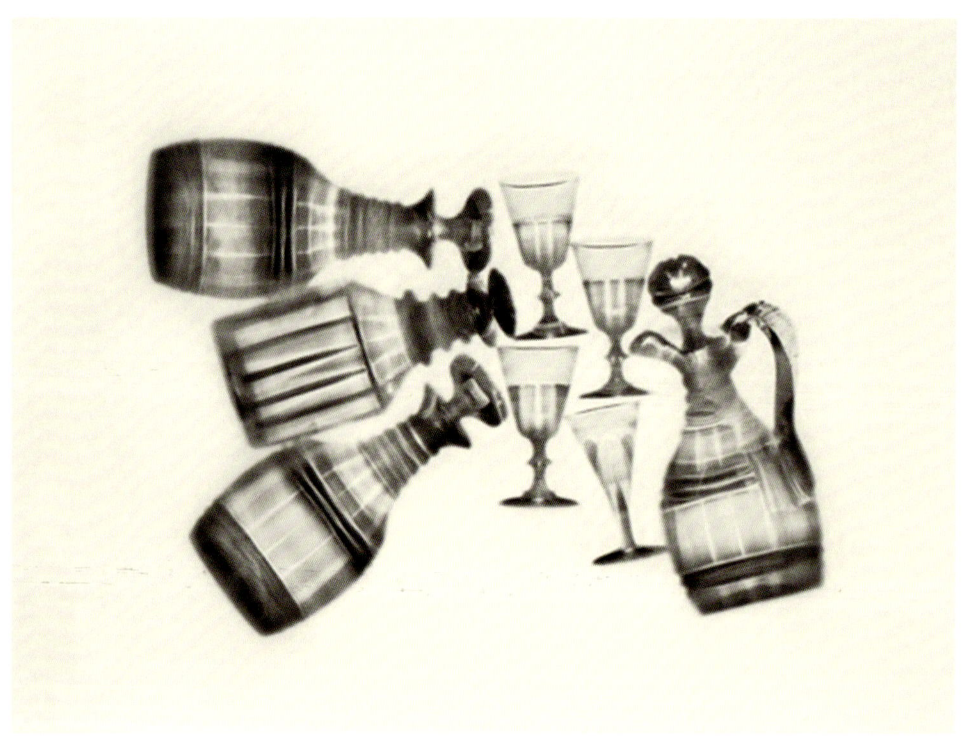

Fox Talbot's Articles of Glass (all that are left) 2016
Photogravure etching on paper, 56.3 × 77.3

fulgurite; the contorted root-like forms are suggestive of the convulsive shock that brought it into being. This naturally occurring alchemy – of sand morphing into glass – resonated with Cornelia Parker who, in 1996, exhibited a piece of fulgurite as a found object. Parker's practice has long been concerned with the transmutability of matter. She investigates the limitations of materials, the potential of objects and their propensity to transform. Rooted in everyday things, which she subjects to (sometimes violent) metamorphosing processes, her work is inflected with an irreverent humour and a literality that cuts to the quick. She plays with dualities – life and death, micro and macro, physical and metaphysical – and is fascinated by things that evade linguistic classification and can 'only be described by [their] opposite':[1] a void quantified by the material that surrounds it; an absence defined by a presence; something that makes nothing perceptible or comprehensible, like a scratch on the surface of a sheet of glass.

Glass became Parker's subject (and object) in 2017, when she made the photogravure series *Fox Talbot's Articles of Glass.* Decoratively cut decanters and wine glasses are arranged in various configurations across the nine prints, ranging from ordered and regimented compositions to those more artfully placed. Framed by the rectangular off-white paper and often surrounded by a considerable amount of negative space, the vessels are unmoored – they appear to be suspended, like a spectral still life. Their prismatic surfaces are articulated in sumptuous greyscale. A shallow depth of field means that certain points are in razor-sharp focus, whilst others soften and recede, their shifting tonal nuances captured in hazy detail. It is as though the images are not fixed to the page at all, but might drift away or dissolve into the support. The series was inspired by the work of photographic pioneer William Henry Fox Talbot, the processes he discovered, and specifically his early photograph

Articles of Glass. Talbot's photograph captures 19 pieces of his glassware collection, arranged across three shelves. Positioned symmetrically and equally spaced in a methodical, melodic rhythm, the tumblers, flutes, dishes and decanters are captured glistening against a black backdrop, 'impress[ing] the sensitive paper with a very peculiar touch'.[2] The articles in Talbot's nineteenth-century photo and those in Parker's series are one and the same – she borrowed the eight surviving glassware pieces of Talbot's collection from the Bodleian Library in Oxford, where they are now housed, and 're-activated them' in print.[3]

Articles of Glass is the fourth plate in Talbot's book, *The Pencil of Nature* – the earliest commercially printed photographic publication. It went on general sale in 1844, aimed at a public most of whom would never have laid eyes on a photograph before. Talbot felt bound to reassure the reader that the images were 'formed or depicted by optical and chemical means alone, and without the aid of any one acquainted with the art of drawing... they are impressed by Nature's hand'.[4] Containing 24 photographs, which cover a wide variety of subjects from landscapes to sculptural busts, each image is accompanied by an explanatory text describing Talbot's scientific process or hypothesising about the medium's potential, which he foretold with accuracy, predicting the camera's use in cataloguing objects, criminal cases and art. The result of a decade's-worth of work, study and experimentation, the book opens with an autobiographical narrative detailing the twists and turns that led Talbot to his discoveries, now legendary within the history of photography. The notion of fixing an image photographically came to him whilst he was honeymooning in Lake Como, Italy, where he became frustrated sketching the picturesque landscape with the aid of a Wollaston Camera Lucida – an early tool used in draughtsmanship that refracts light through a glass prism to generate an optical mirage, so the

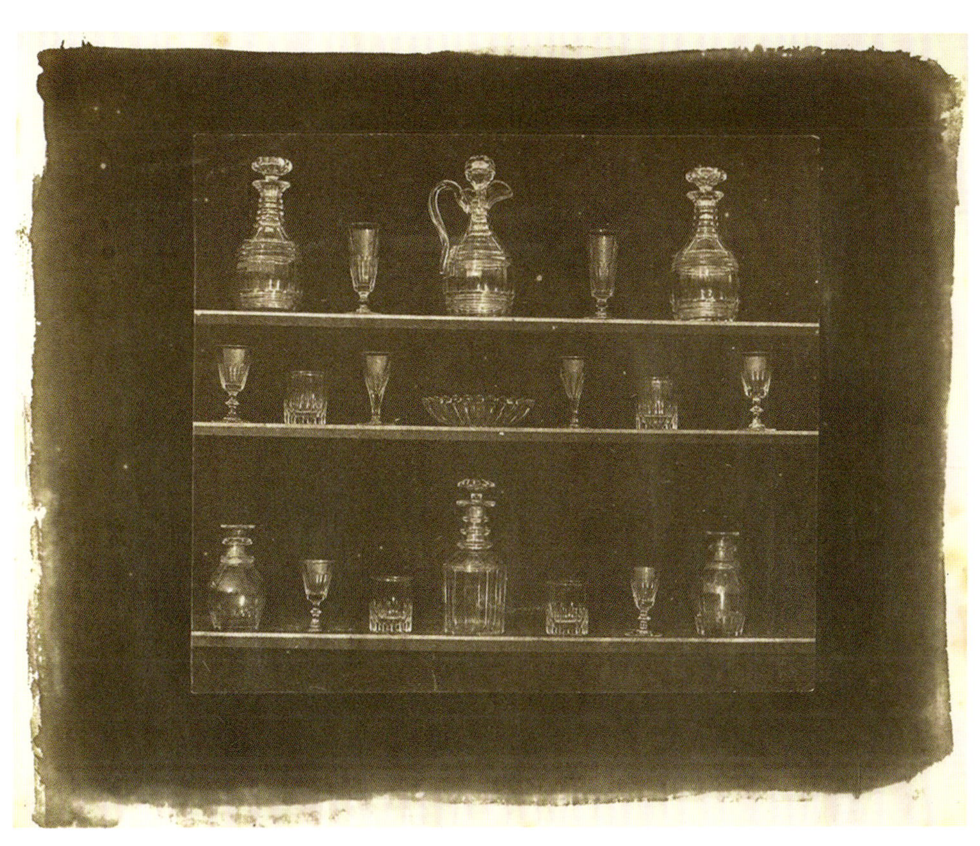

William Henry Fox Talbot
Articles of Glass 1844
Salted paper print, 13.2 × 15.1

scene in front appears to be projected onto the page below. The results were far from satisfactory; Talbot simply couldn't draw. Devoid of texture or tone, variation in the density of line or indication of depth, his drawing was a naively traced outline, lacking artistic skill and sensibility. The event caused him to reflect on the 'fairy pictures' cast by the camera obscura, which he had worked with ten years earlier, and to imagine 'how charming it would be if it were possible to cause these natural images to imprint themselves durably, and remain fixed upon the paper'.[5]

Upon returning home to Lacock Abbey in 1834, Talbot began his photographic experiments in earnest. He quickly discovered that he was able to make paper light-sensitive by coating it with washes of table salt (sodium chloride) and silver nitrate, which created the light-reactive chemical compound silver chloride. Using this process he was able to create some of the first ever photograms by laying opaque, two-dimensional items – often flora and fauna – onto treated paper and exposing it to sunlight. The areas that were covered by the object, and so obscured from light, remained unaltered, whilst those that were exposed turned dark, inscribing the shape of the object onto the paper in an inverted silhouette. Talbot termed these experiments 'photogenic drawings' or *sciagraphs*, literally 'drawing with shadows'. Through trial and error, a year later he succeeded in stabilising these images, making them light-fast by bathing them in a strong solution of common salt, and so the photographic negative was born. This major breakthrough was a milestone in photographic development, setting Talbot's work apart from that of his contemporaries, and led to the production of positive prints he termed *caleotypes*, and which his friends affectionately called Talbotypes.[6] However, the irregular quality of the prints and their tendency to fade caused Talbot to abandon this project a few years after publishing *The Pencil of Nature* (which had

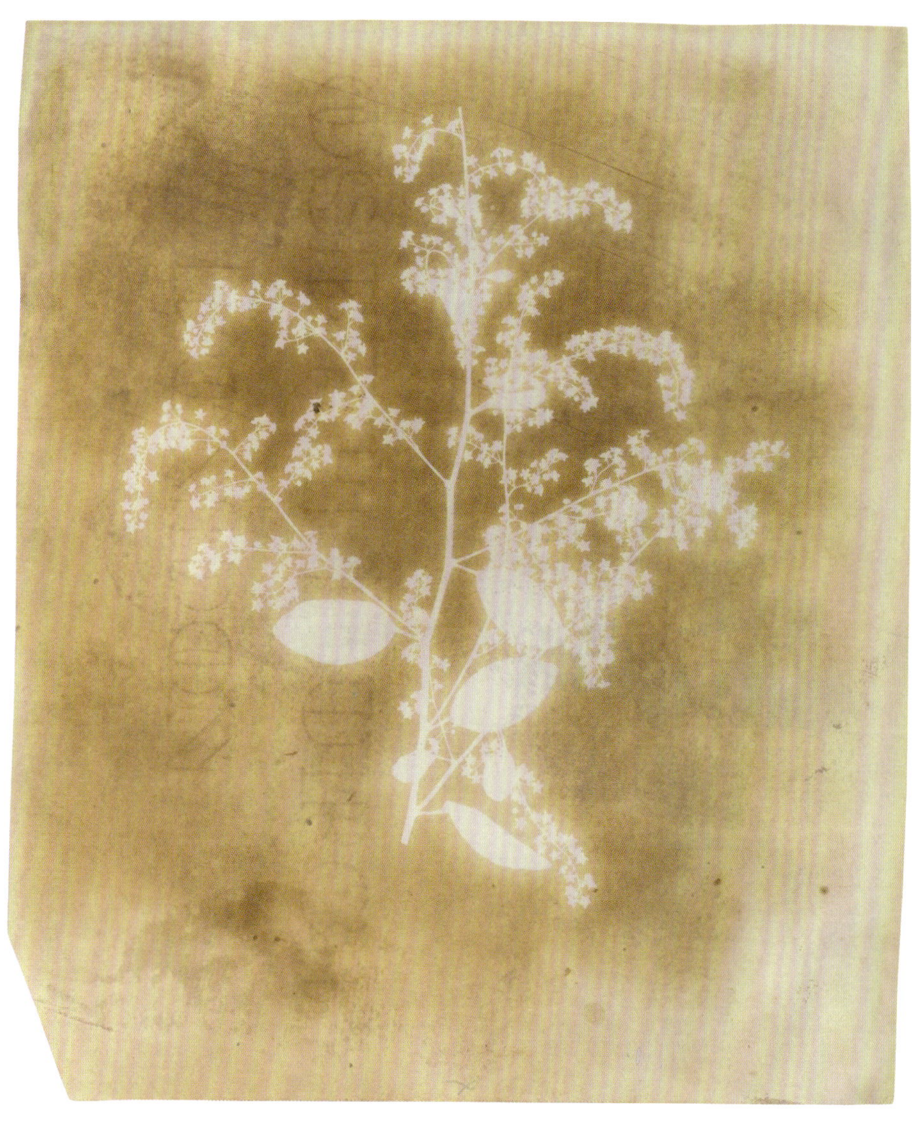

William Henry Fox Talbot
Photogenic Drawing of a Plant 1839–40
Salted paper print, 21.4 × 18.2

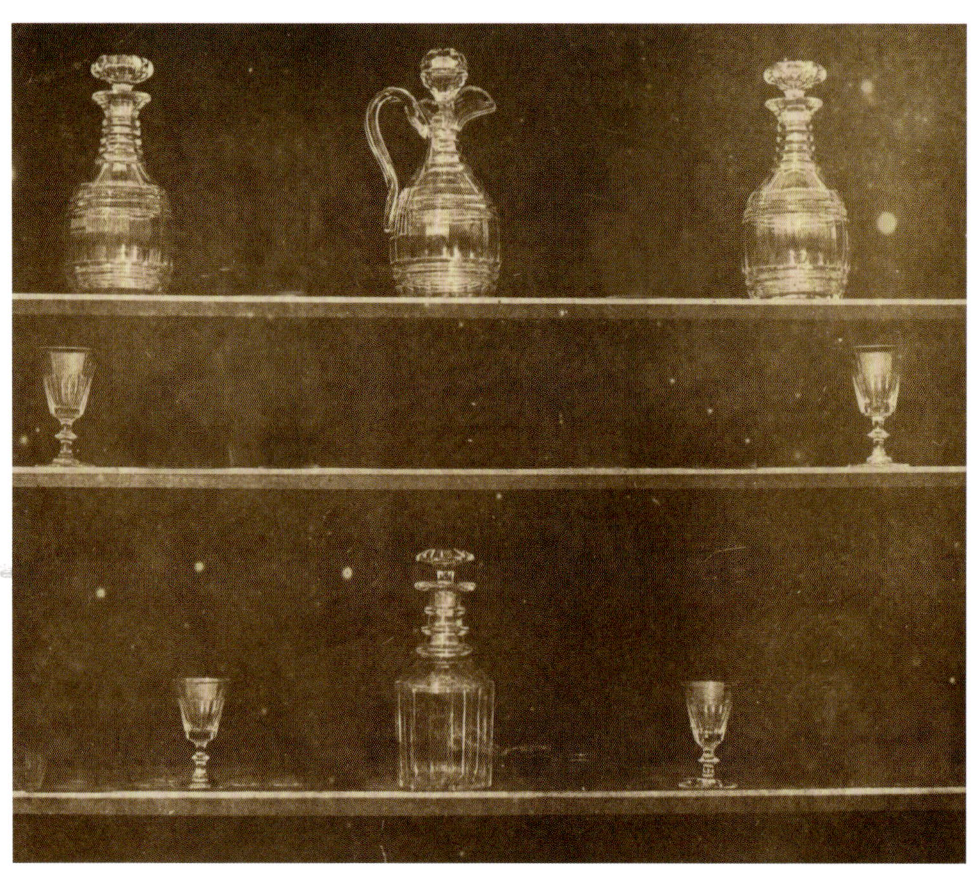

All That Remain 2017
William Henry Fox Talbot's **Articles of Glass** 1844 (plate IV from *The Pencil of Nature*) with all items that are broken or lost removed by Cornelia Parker

been plagued by numerous production problems). By 1850 he was exploring the printing of photographic images with ink, and he dedicated the last 25 years of his life to developing this technique, the *photoglyphic engraving*, which gave rise to the photomechanical printmaking process, the photogravure.

Ever interested in the way that things come into being and the means by which they change, Parker's *Fox Talbot's Articles of Glass* doesn't simply appropriate Talbot's glassware, it uses his photographic processes too. Merging his sciagraphs and photogravure techniques, she has created a hybrid form of printmaking using three-dimensional objects; by placing Talbot's historical glassware directly onto a chemically coated photogravure plate and exposing it to ultraviolet light, she casts shadows of the wine glasses and decanters onto the polymer at a one-to-one scale, like an analogue scan. Where light is able to penetrate the glass, the chemicals on the plate harden, whilst the areas in shadow do not. The unhardened sections are bitten away by acid, generating recesses and incisions in the plate, which, once inked up, produce the velvety prints. Articulated through the shadows cast by Talbot's physical glassware, the prints become a trace, or indexical reference of the objects, and Talbot becomes a referent too, as does his *Articles of Glass*. A 'reactivating', is how Parker describes it, as she resurrected the glassware from its dark storage, some pieces still wearing their museum labels, and literally brought it to light.[7]

Another of Parker's works, also from 2017, draws upon Talbot's photograph *Articles of Glass*. For *All That Remain* she digitally doctored his original print, redacting the glass objects that have since been lost. What remains is a haunting image, though not because the surviving glasswear appears phantasmatic. Rather the obverse is true; the articles stand as a testament, or monuments, to

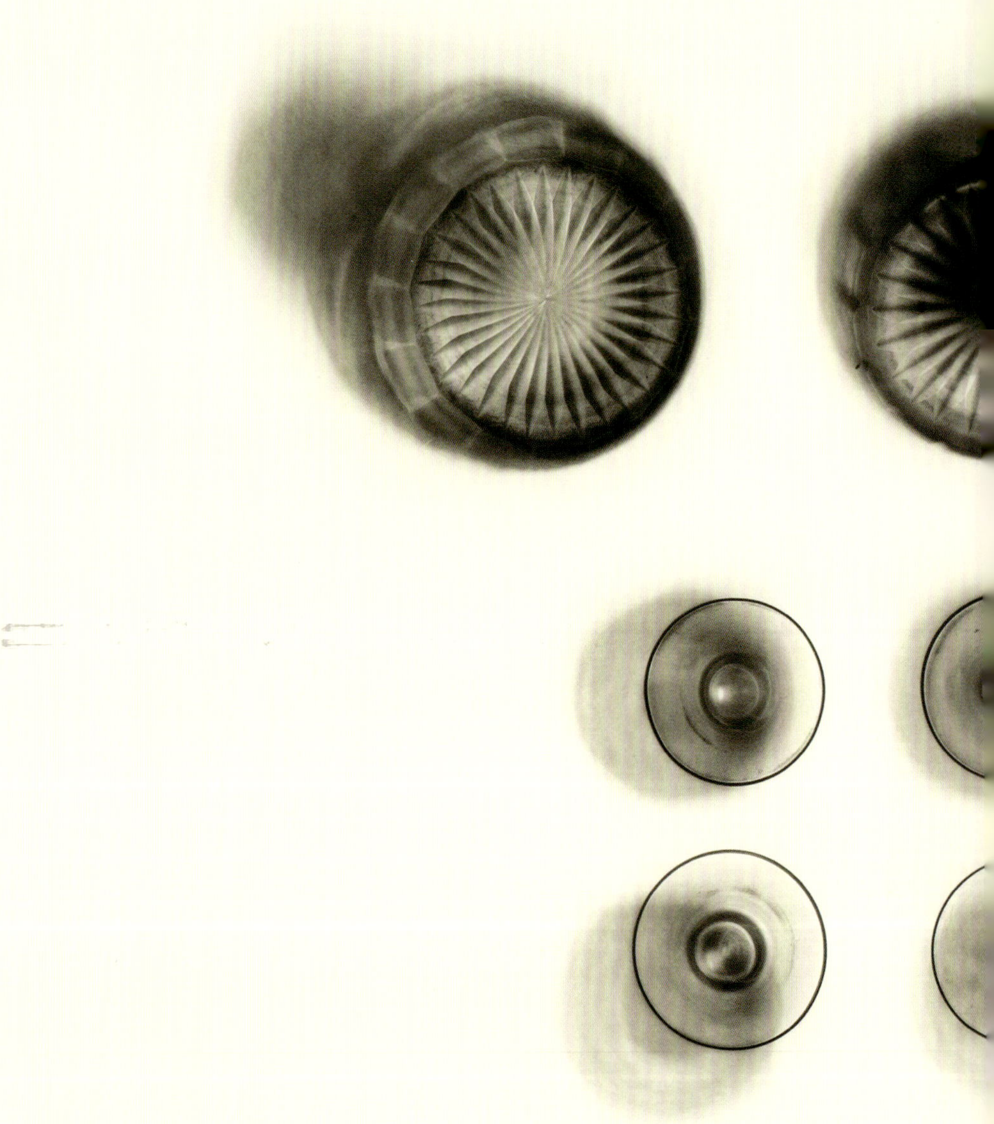

Fox Talbot's Articles of Glass (bottoms up) 2016
Photogravure etching on paper, 56.3 × 77.3

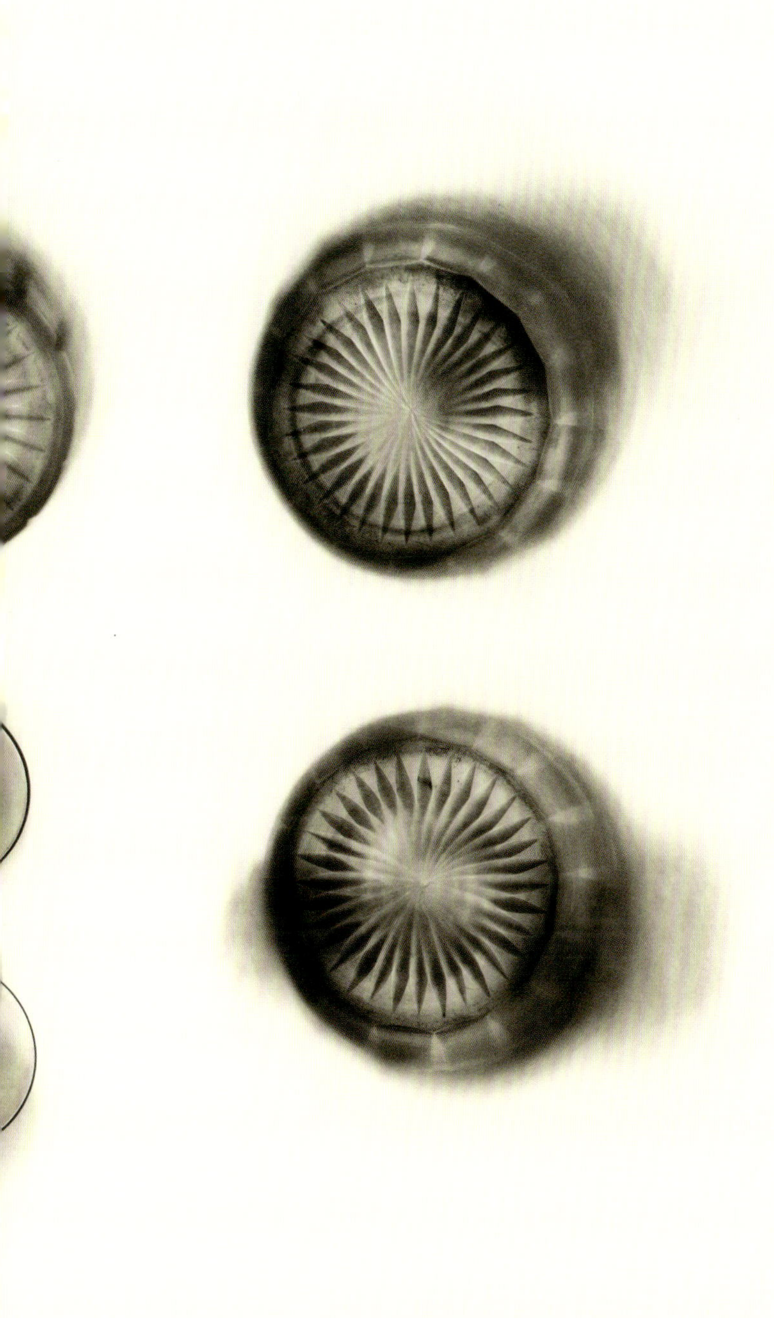

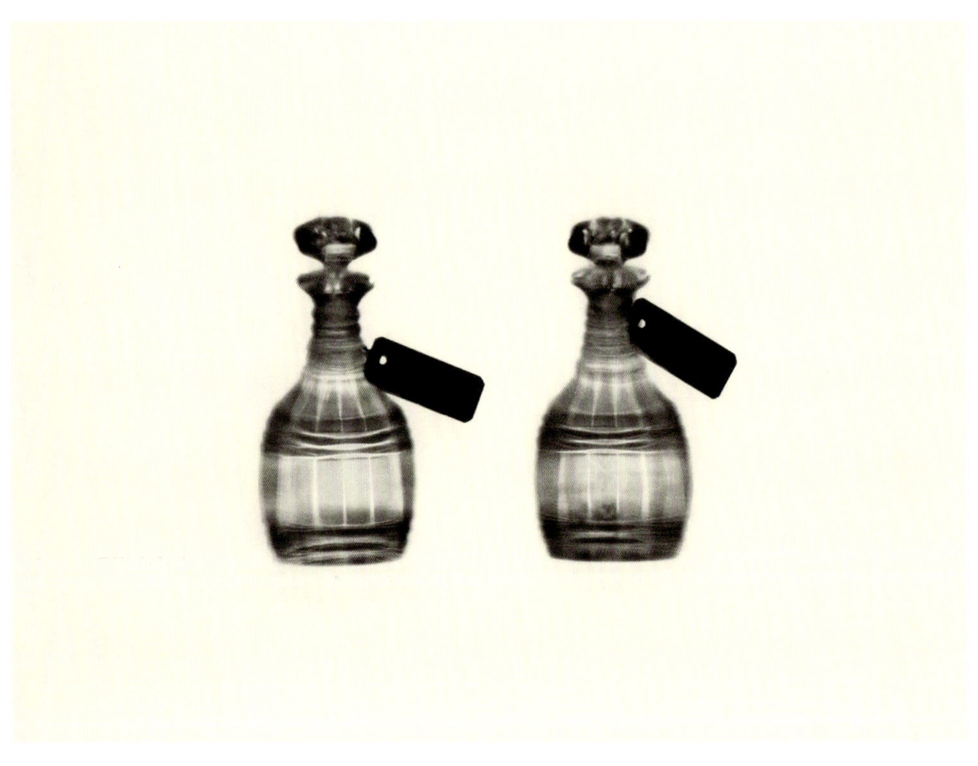

Fox Talbot's Articles of Glass (tagged decanters) 2017
Photogravure etching on paper, 56.3 × 77.3

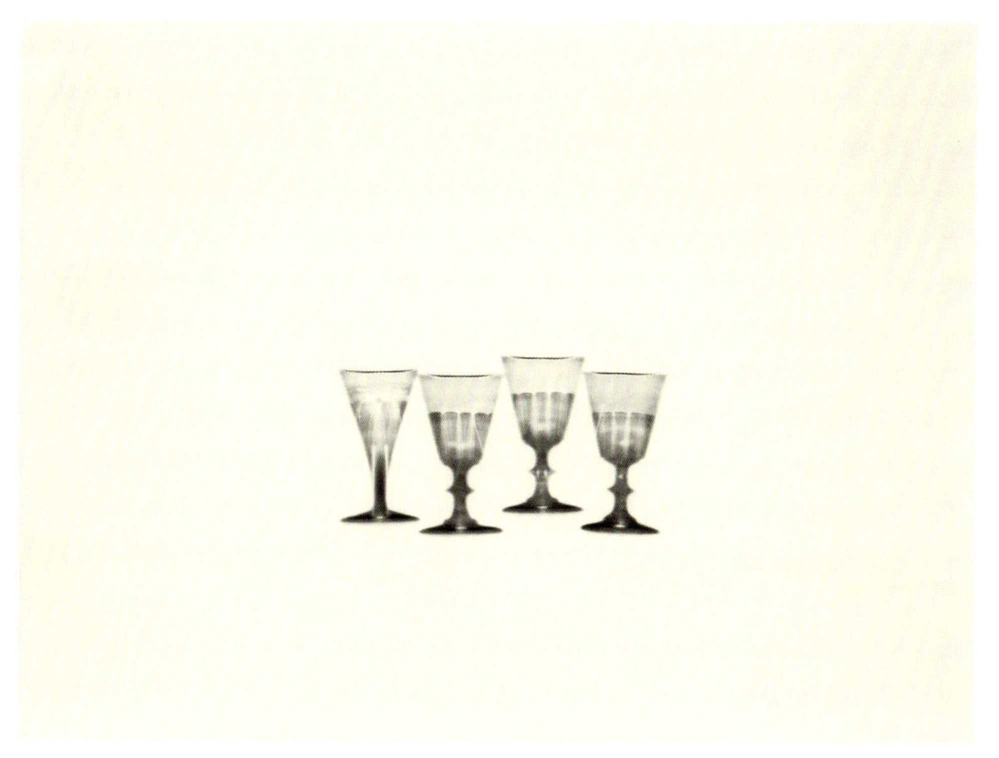

Fox Talbot's Articles of Glass (four glasses) 2017
Photogravure etching on paper, 56.3 × 77.3

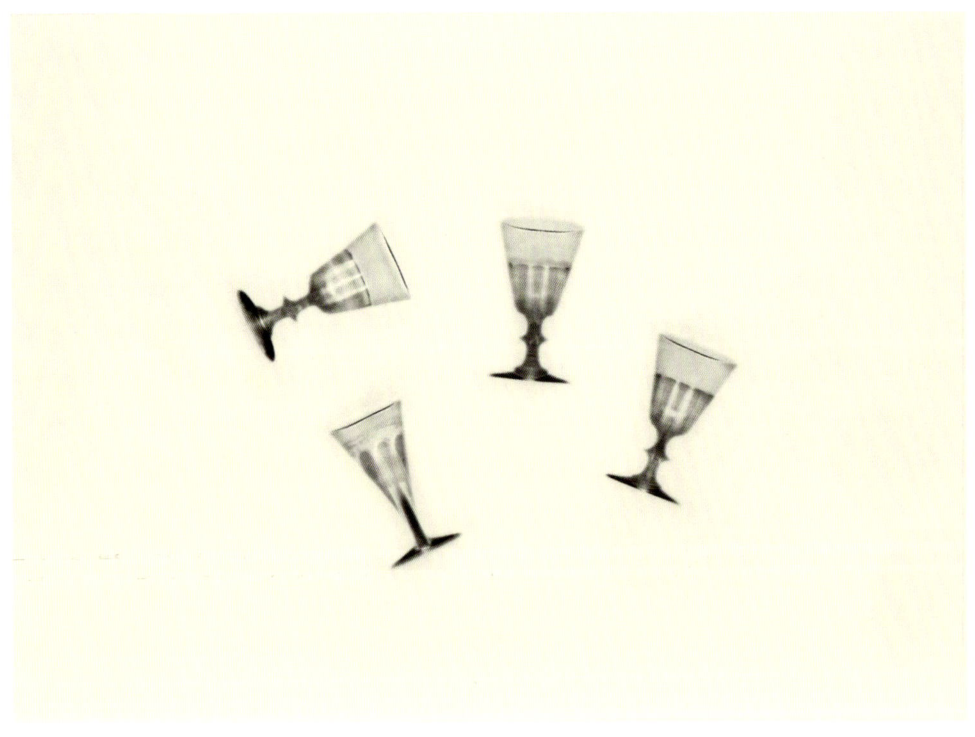

Fox Talbot's Articles of Glass (four glasses more) 2017
Photogravure etching on paper, 56.3 × 77.3

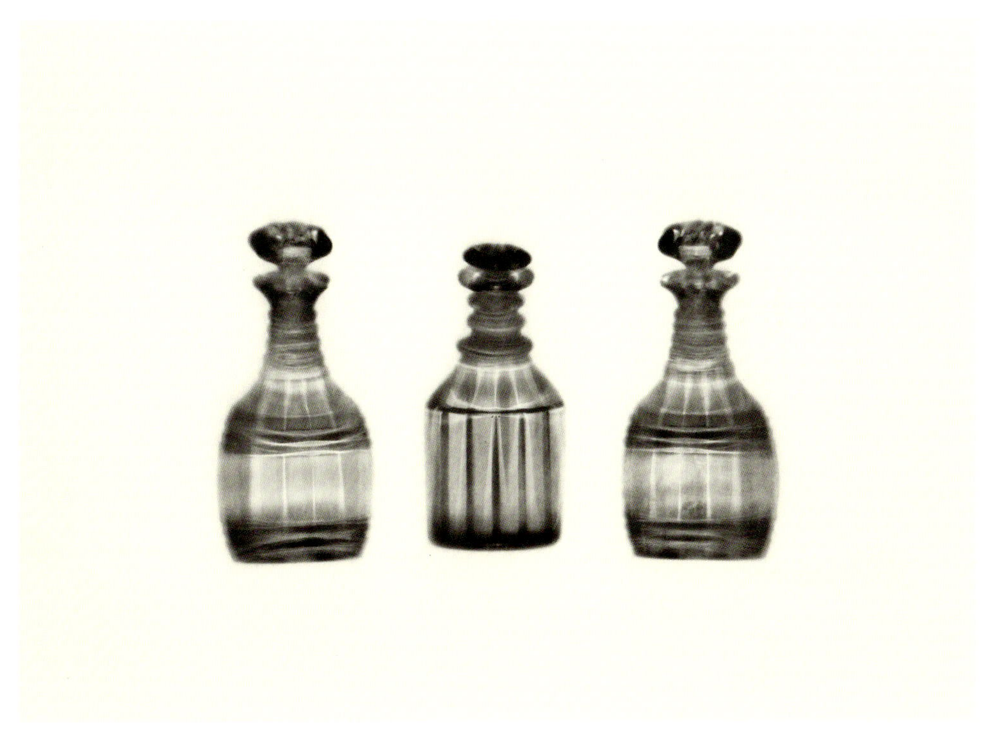

Fox Talbot's Articles of Glass (three decanters) 2017
Photogravure etching on paper, 56.3 × 77.3

the empty spaces on the now sparsely populated shelves. Somehow those absent and those present are both equally visible, as are both analogue and digital technologies – nineteenth and twentieth centuries closing in on each other. In *All That Remain* and her series *Fox Talbot's Articles of Glass* we see Parker take an article from the past and reincarnate it. Histories are accumulated and layered like a palimpsest, pressurising the notion of linear time.

'There are three layers of time' in the series *Thirty Pieces of Silver (Exposed)*, Parker has explained: 'the age of the antique objects, the 1960s when the photographic negatives were taken, and the present, when they are being made into photogravures'.[8] In the 1990s she found a pile of glass 10 × 12-inch negatives in a market in Brick Lane, East London, which detailed the contents of a silverware auction for a Spinks catalogue, one item per negative. They piqued her interest partly because of their relationship to Talbot's images of *Articles*; when she was at art school in the 1970s she had a postcard of *Articles of Silver* tacked to her wall, an image that was choreographed in much the same way as *Articles of Glass*. Parker chose one of these Spinks negatives as the starting point for her first foray into her hybrid form of photogravure printmaking. Treating it as an object she placed it, still encased in its protective glassine bag, onto the photogravure printing plate and exposed it. The process generated an almost tautological print: a negative image of a negative object (pp. 25, 39, 41). The accumulated detritus and damage to glass and the creases and tears of the semi-opaque glassine are clearly rendered in ink; a two-dimensional image of three-dimensional silverware that had been flattened and transubstantiated into a glass object. We see the silver article move through mediums, 'one material becom[ing] another', and are prompted to question the boundaries and borders of an object.[9] Where does an object end and where does it begin? What is its intrinsic essence and what semiotic

Pierced Basket 2015
from **Thirty Pieces of Silver (Exposed)**
Photogravure etching on paper, 66.3 × 54.3

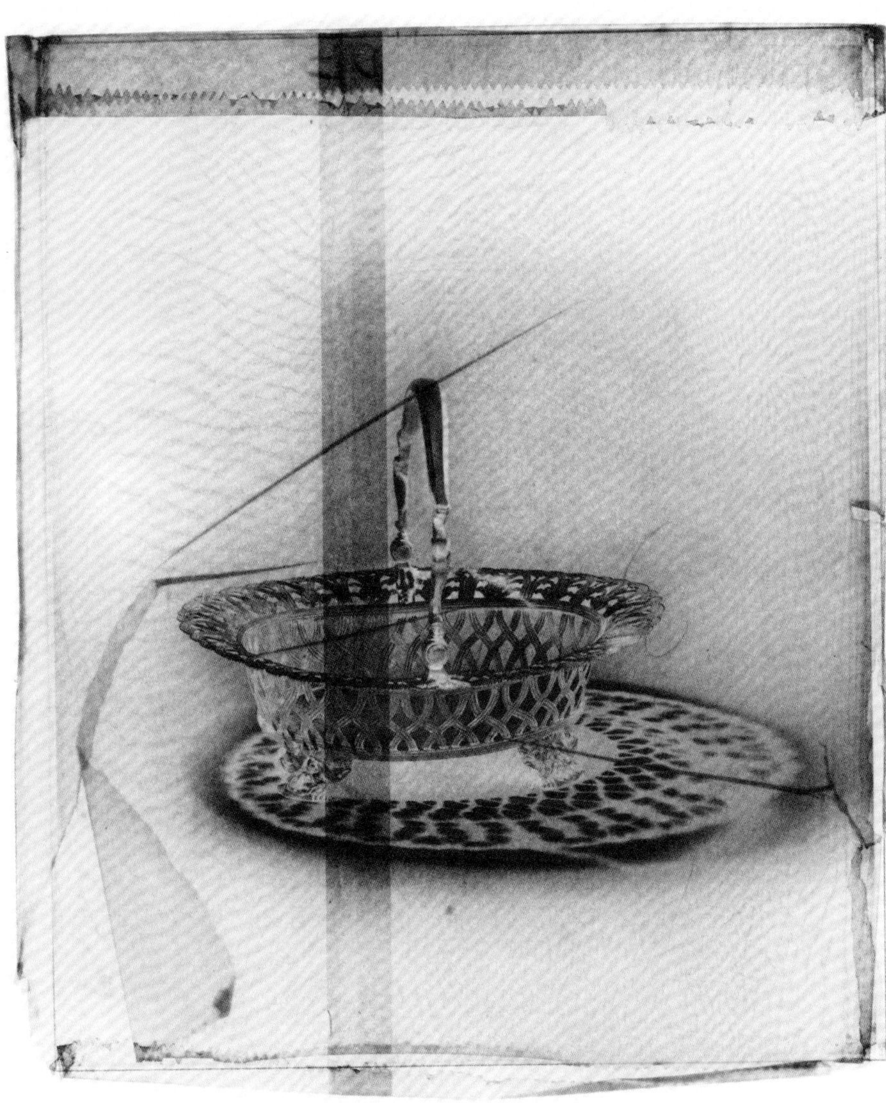

conditions cause it to be a carrier of meaning? What makes a thing a thing?

Nowhere is Parker's curiosity and experimental approach to materials clearer than in her series *One Day This Glass Will Break*, for which she spent five weeks going 'on an adventure' with master printmaker Pete Kosowicz at Thumbprint Editions, testing the possibilities of her new print technique.[10] Parker's insatiable inquisitiveness and her open-ended manner of making and selecting her materials shares an affinity with Talbot. His polymath mind is matched by her eclecticism. Talbot – mathematician, Classics scholar, scientist and photographic pioneer – couldn't draw but called his photographic discovery 'Art' and predicted its value as an artistic medium; Parker – an internationally renowned artist – reads more about science than she does about art, by her own admission.[11] They share an innate ability to work intuitively, responsively and imaginatively, engaging directly with physical matter to discover rather than invent. The series *One Day This Glass Will Break* exemplifies this manner of working; the items captured range from a smashed light bulb to spat-out tequila, indicating the fervour with which they were created.

Black Ice from *One Day This Glass Will Break* depicts the slip and slide of ice cubes across the polymer plate as the UV light caused them to melt during a five-minute exposure. Where water has diluted the chemicals, trails and grey rings are left, marking the slow languishing movements of the solid forms as they change from state to state, returning to liquid once more. The organic globular shapes signal time passing, calling attention to the duration of the exposure. If you look closely at the print it still possible to discern some ice cubes that are shaped as Halloween skull and crossbones –

Black Ice 2015
from **One Day This Glass Will Break**
Photogravure etching on paper, 81.7 × 58

nodding to Vanitas paintings, still lifes (*natures mortes*) and mortality, but also to comic trick-or-treat (pp. 98–99). Here the composition was a happy accident. Parker also took advantage of the horizontal plane of the photogravure plate to artfully choreograph her compositions *Still Life with Levitating Grapes* and *Told You So*, so that fruit appears to float from its bowl and a tower of glasses tumbles, capturing the precariousness of something in transition or a moment of potential (pp. 37, 31).

The 'mantra', as Parker has described it, of 'truth to materials' is ingrained in her artistic approach.[12] But rather than implying faithfulness to the intrinsic properties of objects and substances, Parker pressurises this truth; a deeper epistemological inquiry or subtext seems to be at stake. Her investigations are grounded in the physical stuff of the real world, often paying attention to overlooked everyday items, but she focuses on the seemingly mundane or the micro to open up to the macro – to extraordinary and fundamental existential questions. In expressing the mutability of objects – the inevitability of one thing morphing into another, like sand into glass – and by short-circuiting the forward propulsion of chronological time through layering historical moments, Parker's practice can be understood as a subtle interrogation of the dependent origination of all things and our own place within that system. Nothing can come into existence in isolation. We are reminded that the only thing we can grab hold of in life with any surety is the nature of impermanence. Change is inevitable and our mortality is certain. Nothing is fixed, photographs will eventually fade, and one day this glass will break.

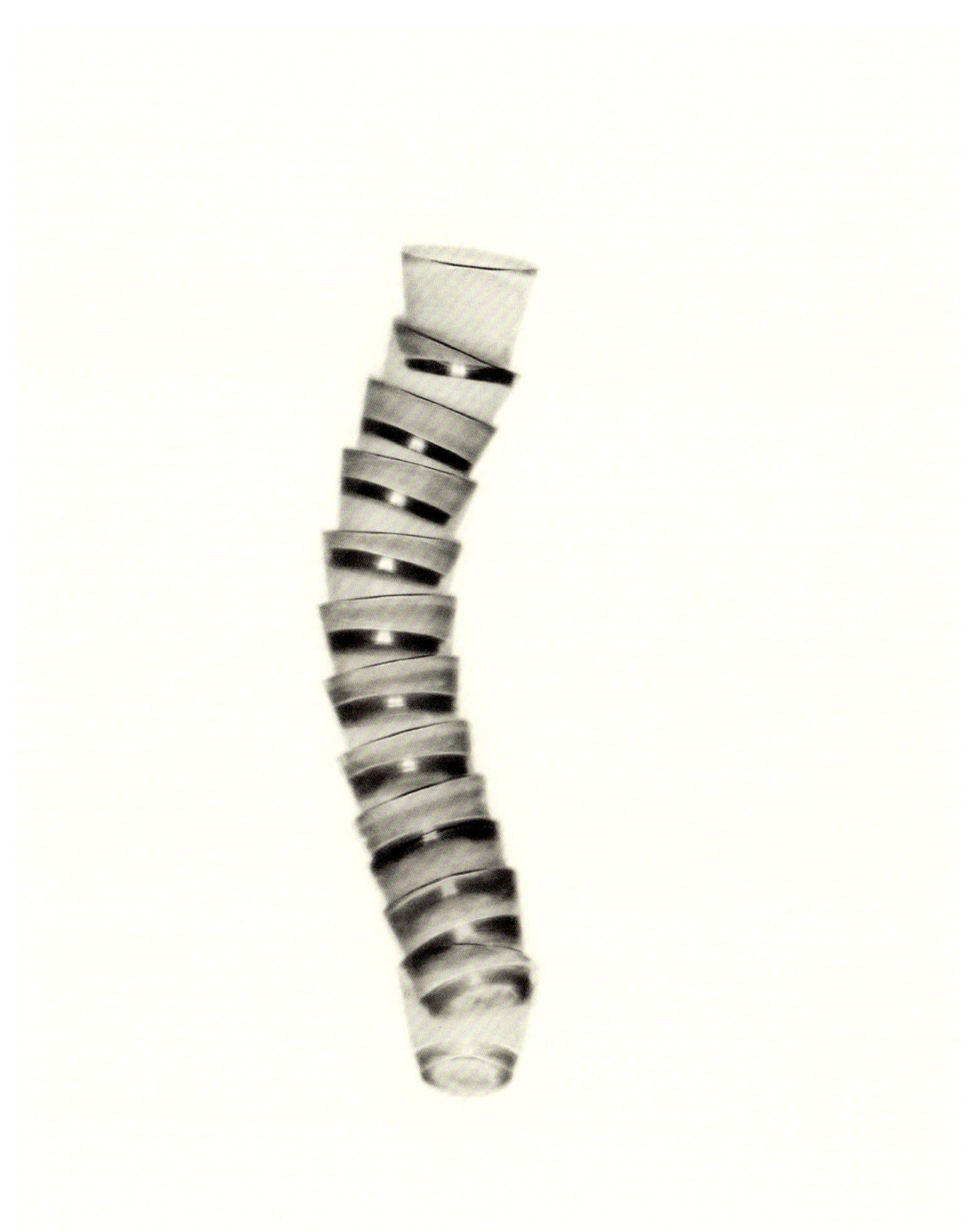

One Day This Glass Will Break 2015
from **One Day This Glass Will Break**
Photogravure etching on paper, 70 × 50

1
Cornelia Parker: Talking Art, Cornelia Parker interviewed by Lisa Le Feuvre, Tate Modern, London, 31 May 2008. Accessed: http://www.tate.org.uk/context-comment/video/cornelia-parker-talking-art

2
William Henry Fox Talbot, *The Pencil of Nature* (New York: Capo Press, 1969), Unpag.

3
Unpublished interview with the artist, whilst preparing the exhibition *One Day This Glass Will Break*.

4
Talbot 1969.

5
Ibid.

6
Talbot was not alone in his pursuit to capture and fix photographic images. Thomas Wedgwood had first discovered the photogram technique by coating leather in silver nitrate, but his images faded as he lacked the knowledge to fix them, while Joseph Nicéphore Niépce and Louis Daguerre were making headway with their experiments with light-sensitive materials.

7
Unpublished interview with the artist, whilst preparing the exhibition *One Day This Glass Will Break*.

8
Helen Waters, Cornelia Parker and Pete Kosowicz, *Cornelia Parker: One Day This Glass Will Break* (London: Alan Cristea Gallery, 2015), p. 8.

9
Ibid., p. 9.

10
Unpublished interview with the artist, whilst preparing the exhibition *One Day This Glass Will Break*.

11
Ibid.

12
Parker interviewed by Le Feuvre.

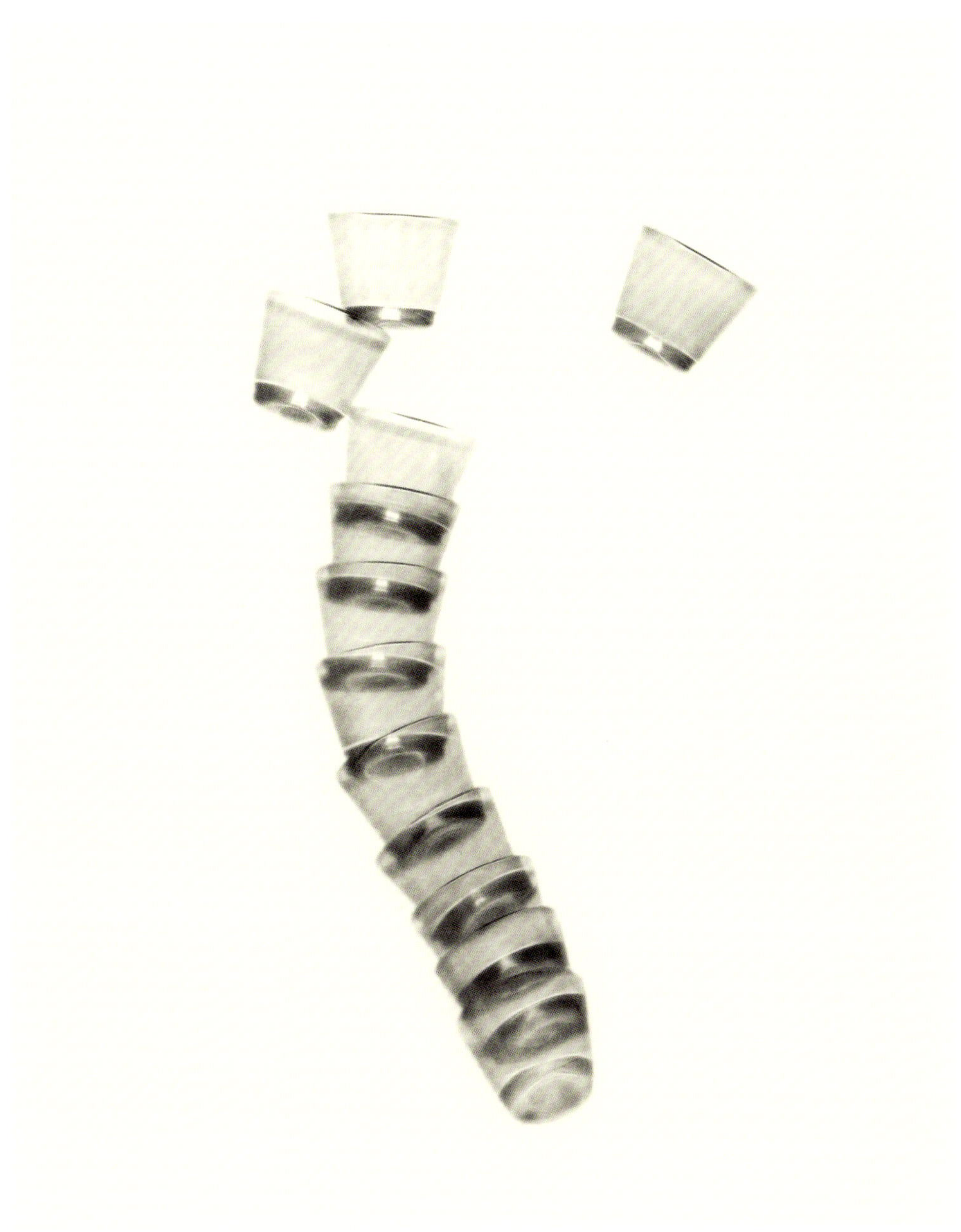

Told You So 2015
from **One Day This Glass Will Break**
Photogravure etching on paper, 70 × 50

An Idea 2015
from **One Day This Glass Will Break**
Photogravure etching on paper, 72.2 × 58

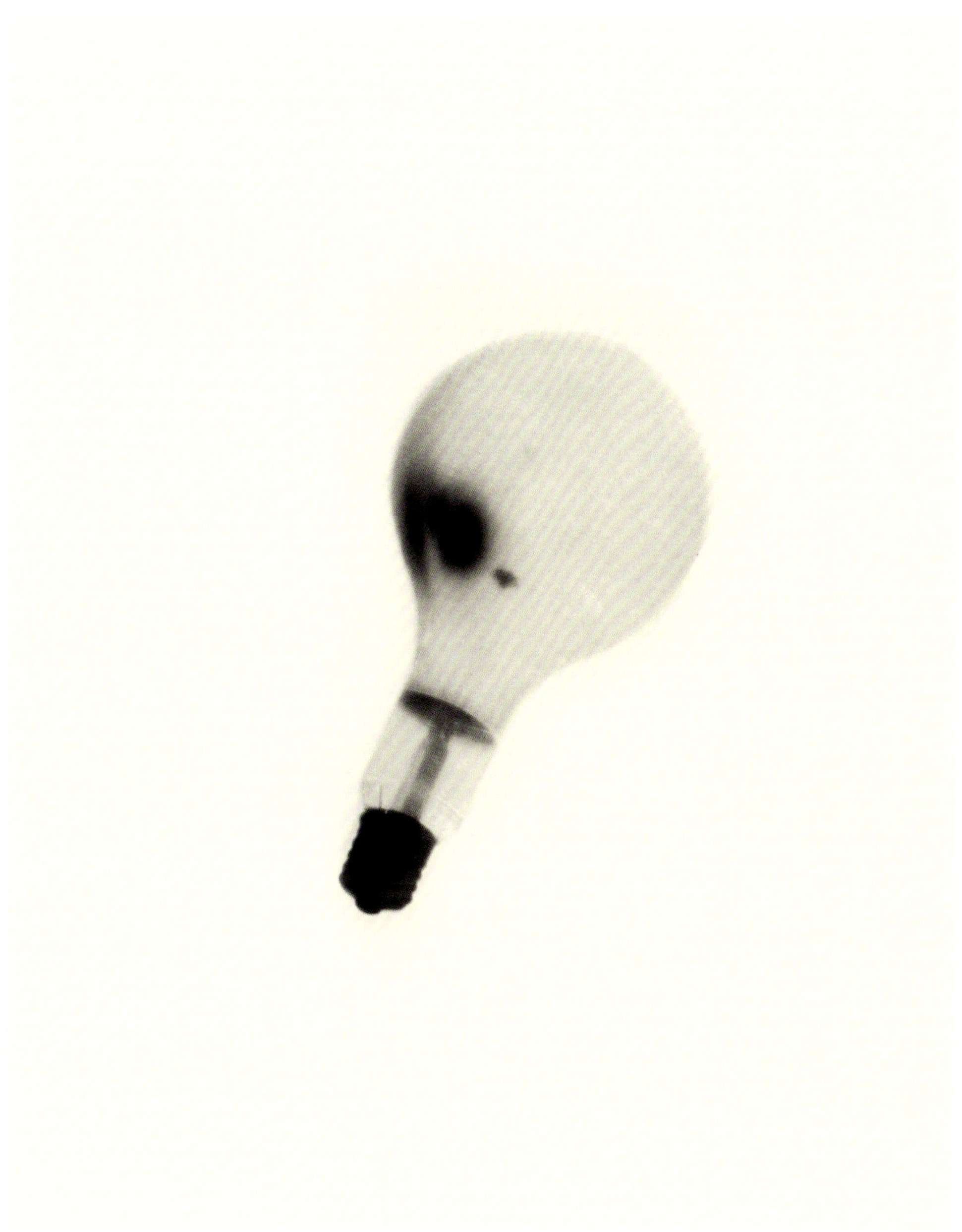

Premeditated Act of Violence 2015
from **One Day This Glass Will Break**
Photogravure etching on paper, 72.2 × 58

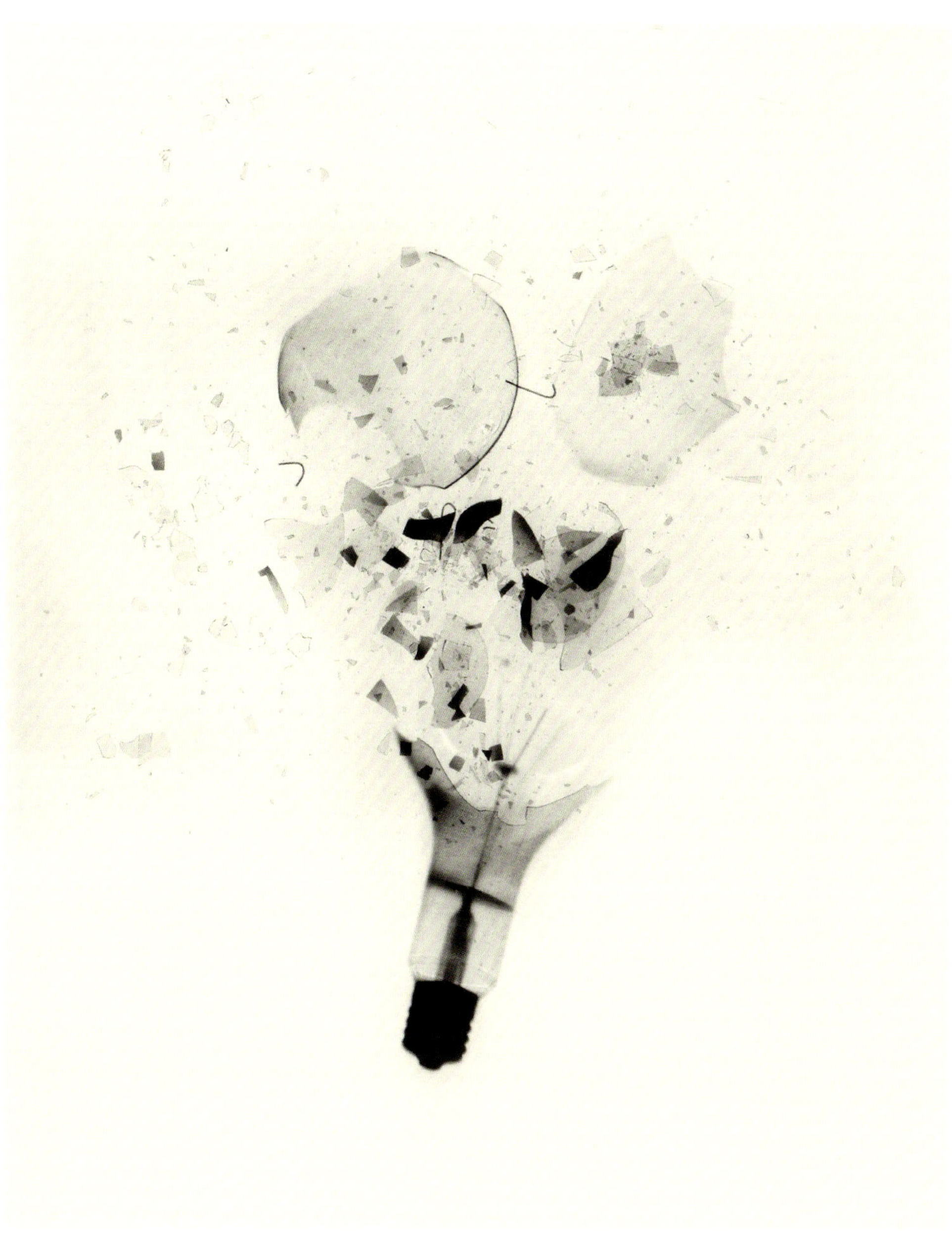

Still Life with Levitating Grapes 2015
from **One Day This Glass Will Break**
Photogravure etching on paper, 72.2 × 54

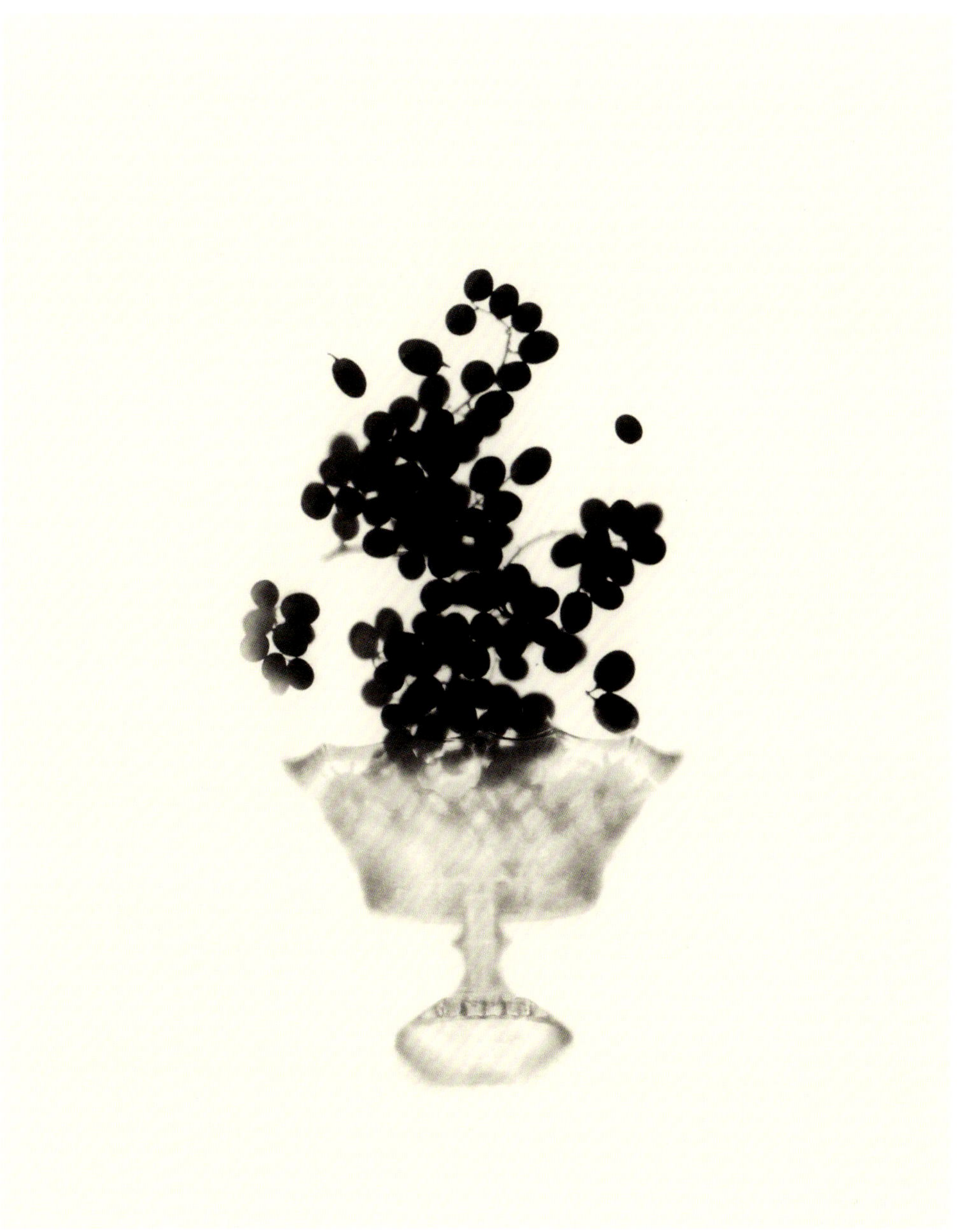

Coffee Pot Hit with a Monkey Wrench 2016
Photogravure etching on paper, 68 × 56

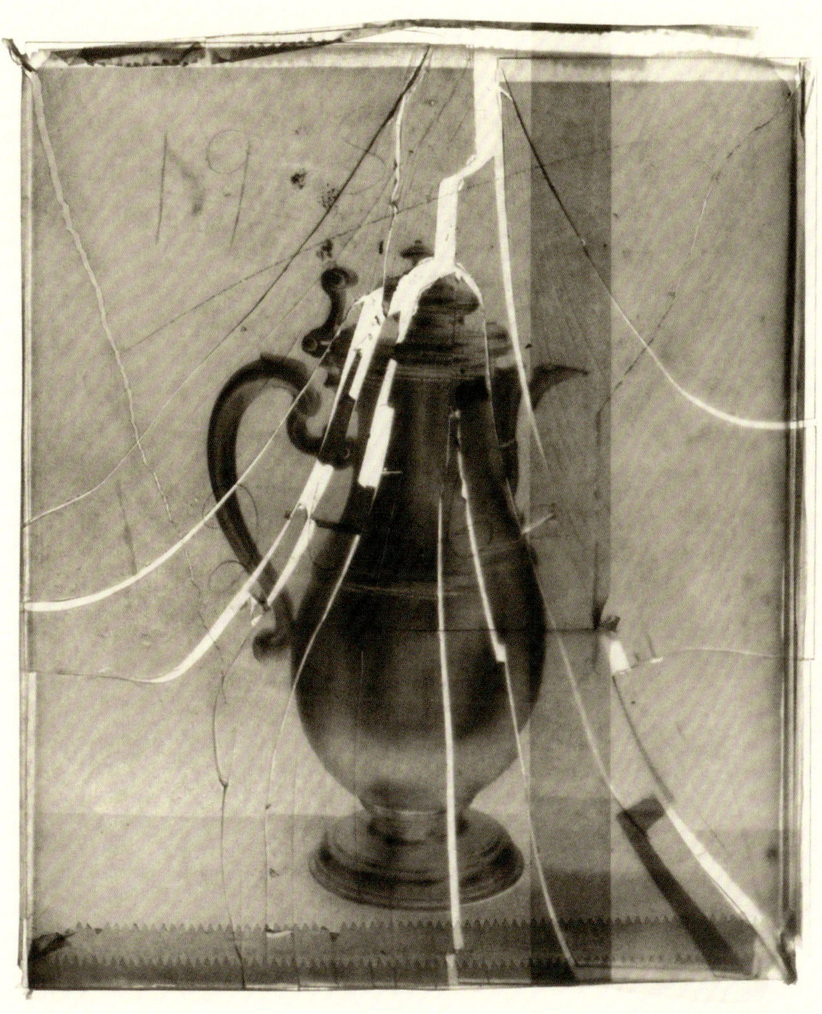

Broken Tureen 2015
from **Thirty Pieces of Silver (Exposed)**
Photogravure etching on paper, 54.3 × 66.3

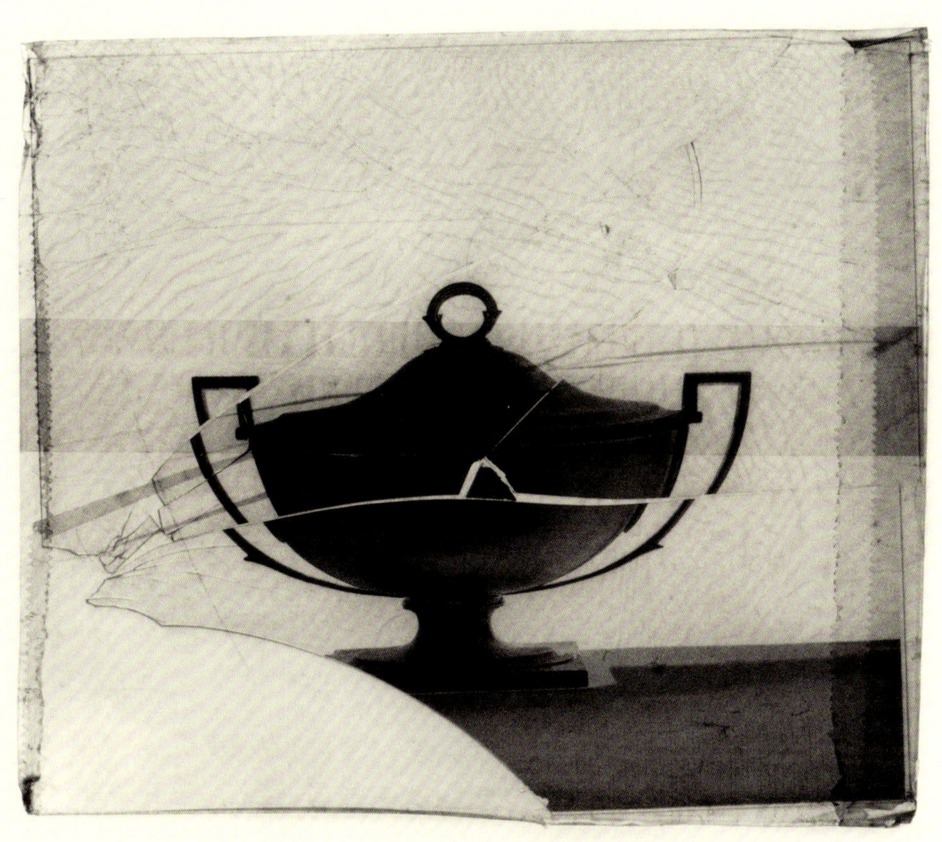

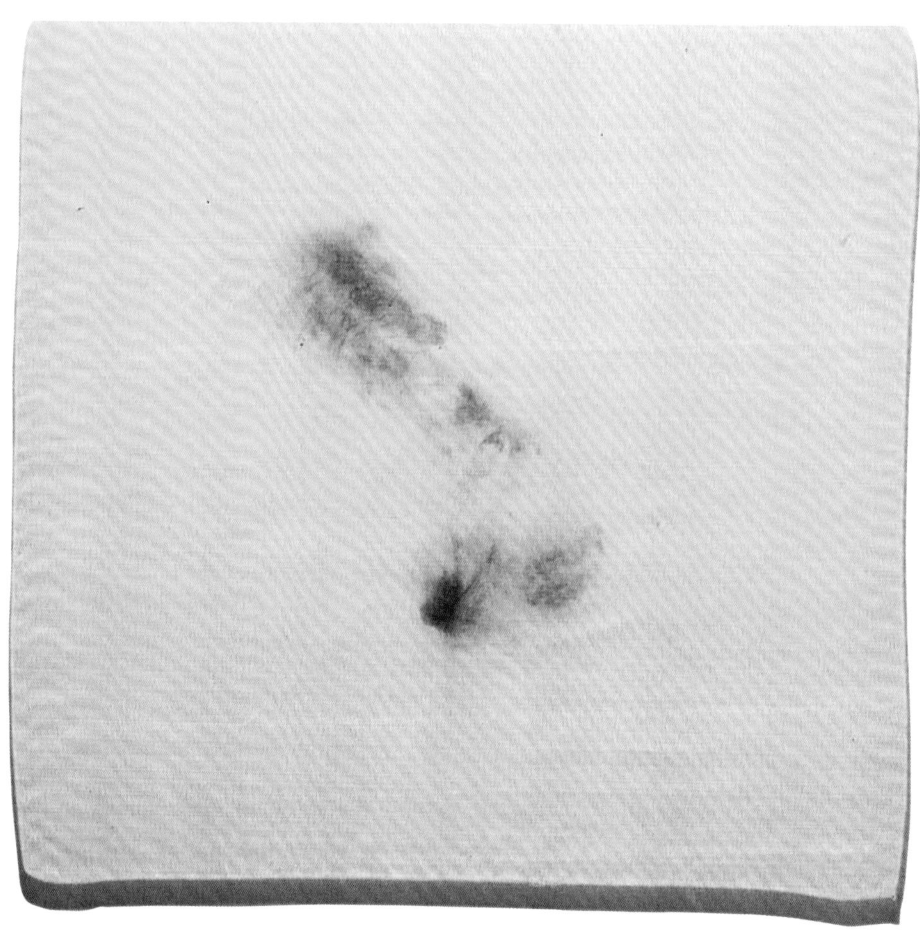

Stolen Thunder: Tarnish from James Bowie's Soup Spoon 1997
(inventor of the Bowie knife)
Oxidised silver on cotton handkerchief, 63 × 63
With thanks to The Alamo, Texas

Stealing Shadows: Cornelia Parker in conversation with David Campany

David Campany Where does your interest in photography come from?

Cornelia Parker It's always been there. I'm especially drawn to early photography and Fox Talbot's idea of the photographic process acting as the 'pencil of nature' (see pp. 12–17). Also, the camera obscura, and the frustration of people not being able to capture what they saw. With everything I make I'm looking at the *way* things are made as I've got no technical expertise...

D ... You're making it up as you go along in the way Fox Talbot was.

C I love a pioneering approach, discovering things for the first time.

D Even when you're not doing something with photography or printmaking, the photographic seems to haunt your work anyway. It might be to do with how you use traces or translations of things, or casts or off-casts of things.

C My relationship with photography is in exploring that territory. For example, I've exhibited the tarnish on handkerchiefs after polishing famous people's silverware, simultaneously taking an impression of an object, gathering a silver trace whilst rubbing away a shadow. Buffing up a tarnished reputation perhaps or capturing an original sin. Silver has this duality that I really love, because it oxidises, chemically reacting to its environment. It is a material I'm consistently drawn to and that's partly due to its links to

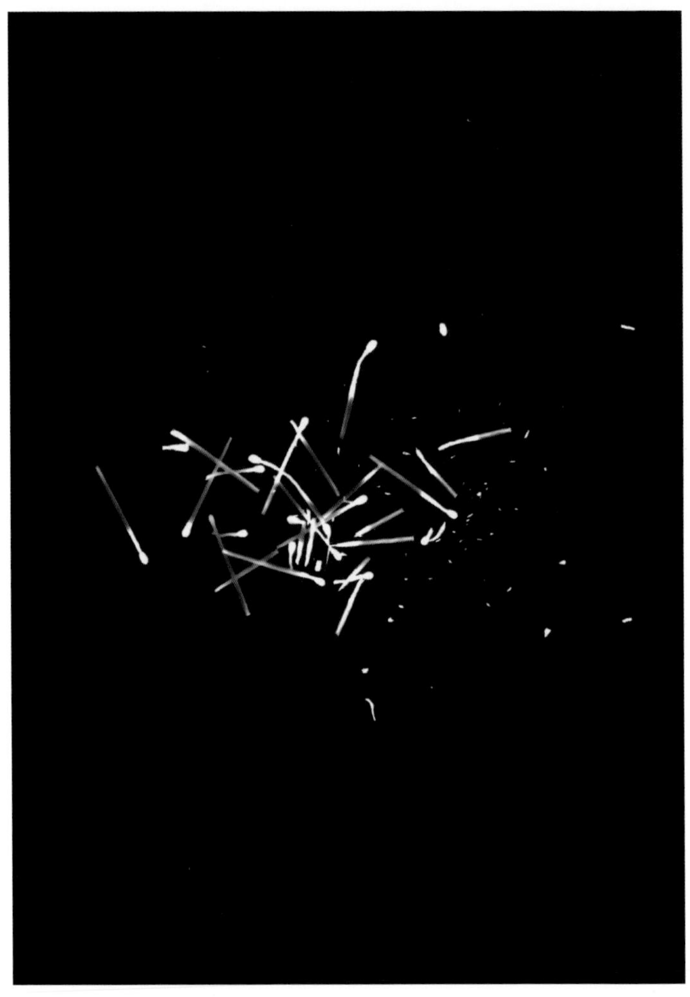

Spent Matches Exposed by a Live One 2001
Photogram, 70 × 60.5

photography, the idea that silver gelatin is affected by shadow, that stopping light allows an impression to be formed.

D With that in mind, I would have thought you'd be just as interested in Daguerre, who didn't use a paper negative like Fox Talbot, but a polished silver surface.

C I like Daguerre, but for me his process is too sealed off, encapsulated, a dead end. I think there's more space for the artist in Fox Talbot because he outlines all the possibilities and you take it where you want. There's also something more scientific, more pragmatic about his process: he formally arranged then catalogued the effects of light falling on objects – ceramics, glass, silver.

D It's uncanny how accurate Fox Talbot was when he outlined all the different ways photography might go. He predicted the artwork, the document, the copy, the complicated status of evidence, cataloguing. His own account is that photography partly comes out of a lousy inability to draw, but he's not commercially minded at all, just very curious.

C He's a maven. Like Duchamp, he moves on when he's found the mechanism, the way something works. I also like to work in lots of different ways, to jump around a lot – otherwise known as attention-deficit disorder!

Alan Cristea invited me to make an exhibition of prints for his gallery, enquiring what kind of ideas I might pursue. Initially ideas might just be decoys, because when you start working you find yourself going off-piste very quickly. I'd done photo-etching before and made photograms in the dark room, but found they had their limitations. For this show, I was trying to find a new way of taking an object and making an image with it.

The experiments I'd made with photograms I started to apply to photogravure, asking, 'What will happen if you put some ice on this photosensitive plate and process it?' There was this instantaneous moment when I emptied the glass jug of ice onto the plate, and then exposed it to light, capturing the gesture as a freeze-frame still life. I expected that the ice's transparency would be revealed, but instead an exciting thing happened; the ice started to chemically react and eat into the gelatin. So instead of appearing transparent, in print the ice cubes became various shade of black, recording the five minutes of the exposure, the rings of the melt (p. 27). When using glass objects in photogravure, anything that sits on the plate's surface is sharply in focus, and everything that's not making contact is more blurred.

D It has the illusion of depth.

C I'm using a combination of Fox Talbot's techniques, sun prints and photogravure. For example, he would lay a two-dimensional object like a leaf or a piece of lace onto a piece of prepared paper and allow the sun to do its work. For capturing three-dimensional objects, he felt he had to develop his ideas further by inventing a camera.

D Fox Talbot was very interested in what happens to the image not when you explain it but when you add something. In the same way, every time I'm at a show of yours, I'm looking for a key somewhere, perhaps a caption, that tells me something that the image cannot tell me. And then the whole piece gets expanded. So, I might be looking at a projected image of a feather, and then you tell me it's from Freud's pillow (overleaf).

C The projection is the light bouncing off the actual feather, which I trapped in a glass slide and then projected anamorphically along

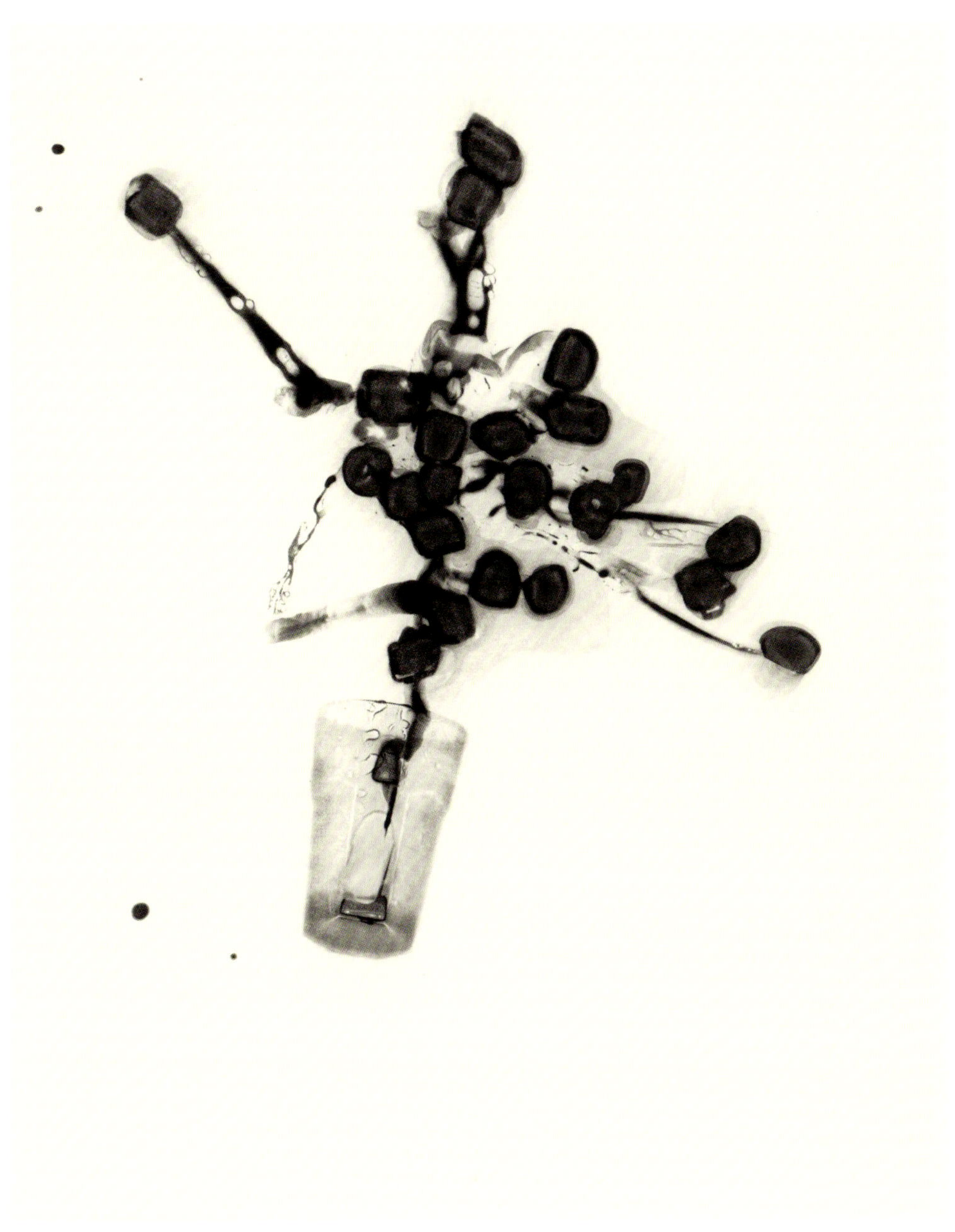

Tumbler with Ice 2015
from **One Day This Glass Will Break**
Photogravure etching on paper, 72.2 × 58

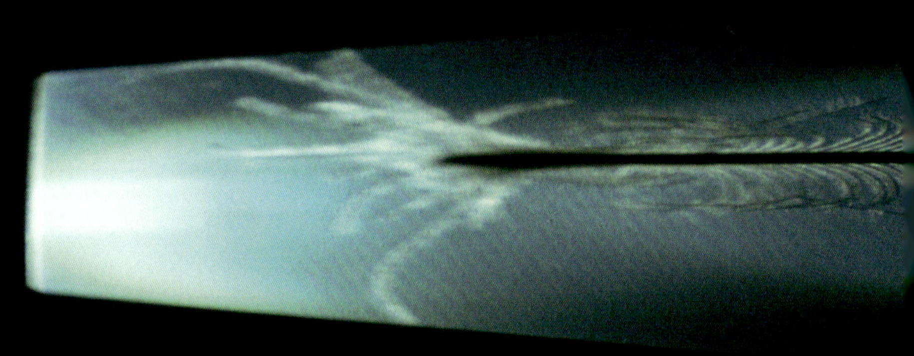

Projection: Feather from Freud's Pillow (From his Couch) 1996
Feather placed in a 35mm glass slide then projected, dimensions variable

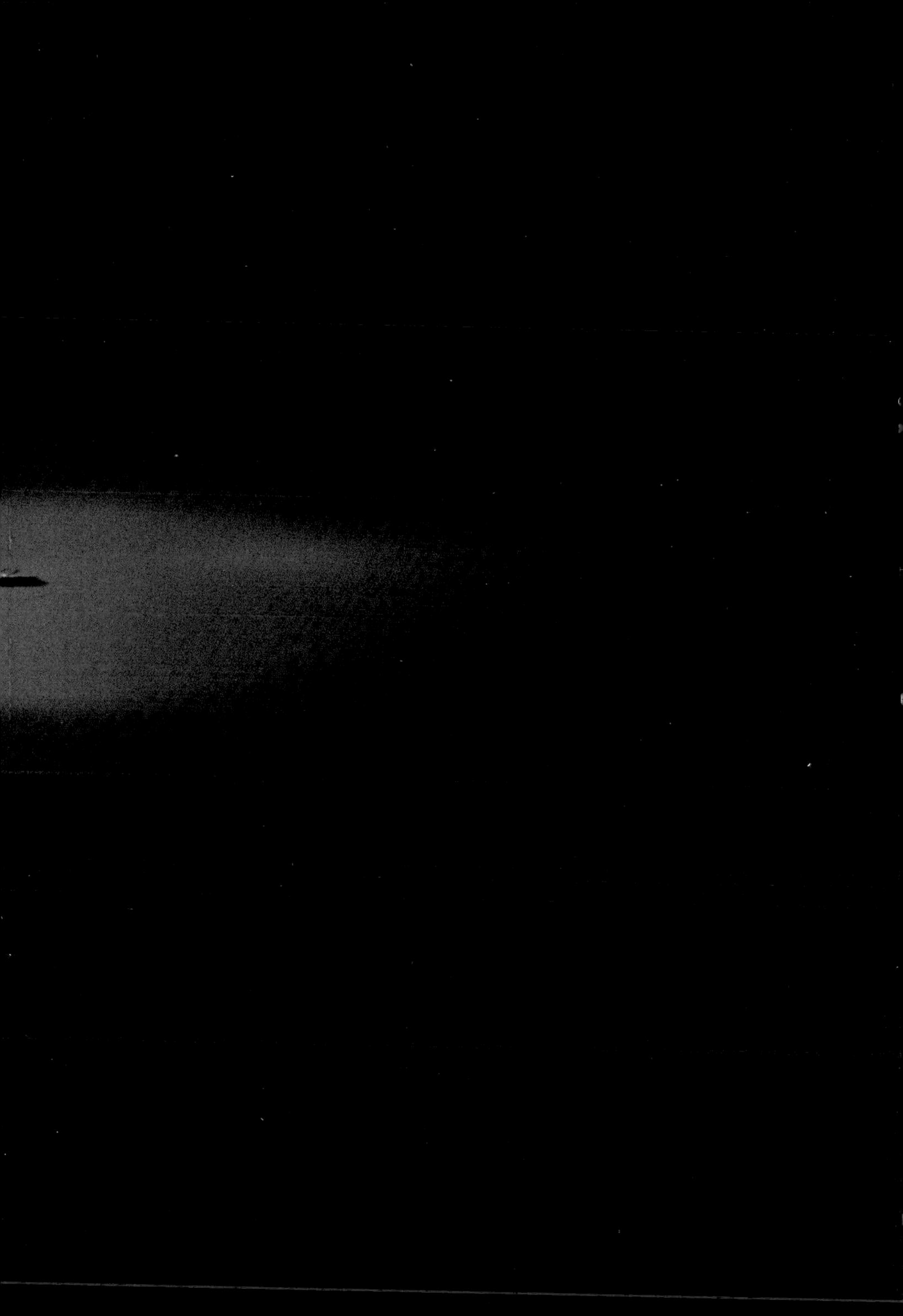

the wall. Suddenly it has a dynamism that it doesn't have when it's been passively sitting in the dark inside Freud's pillow. It looks like an arrow shot from a bow, a tiny broken feather becomes a lethal weapon.

D You also made a really beautiful photograph of the cracked leather seat on Freud's chair, and you describe these marks as being made unconsciously or subconsciously by Freud. I'm led to think that there would be a significance in this – but really it could be arbitrary. That's a tightrope that you obviously like to walk.

C But that's the tightrope that we walk in all our lives, isn't it? We're always looking for tangible meaning, but meaning is a slippery thing. That's the human dilemma, the big question – are we worth something or worthless? I love abrasion, I love wear, and Freud's chair, with all those creases made by his bottom, not by his head or his intellect, seemed to reveal the underbelly of this huge myth. The photograph acts as a kind of cartography drafting Freud's subconscious.

D The captions giving the source of the feather, or cause of the cracked leather seat, seem to indicate that the thing itself, the object itself or the trace itself, in the end relies on language, not to explain it but to open it up.

C If you didn't have a caption beside a newspaper photograph it would become unmoored. Photography either with or without the caption works in different ways. Take my image of a pinhole made by Charlotte Brontë, which I made with an electron microscope: it looks like an abyss, like the end of the universe, like a black hole, but when you've read the title, you realise it's just a tiny pinhole made unconsciously by the author of these iconic books (p. 55). It's a

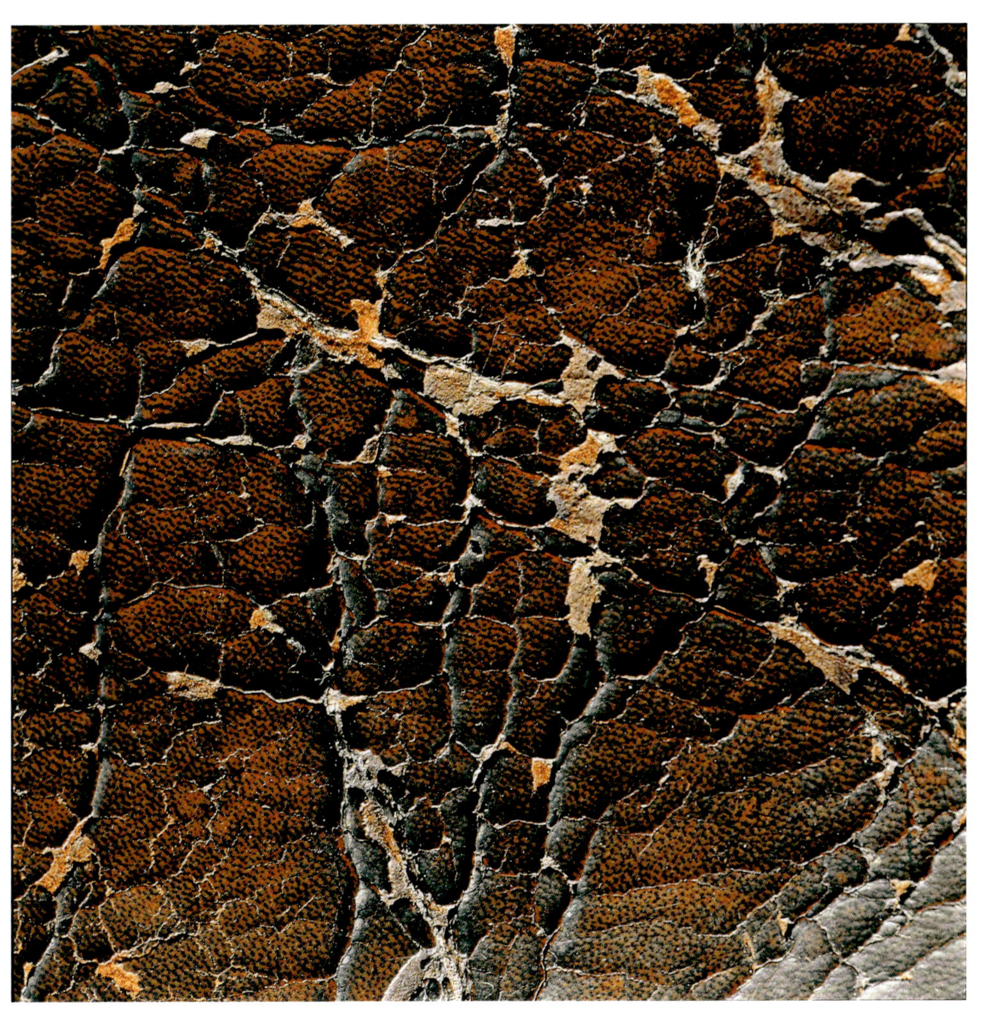

Marks Made by Freud, Subconsciously 2000
Cibachrome, macro-photo of Freud's leather chair, 63 × 63

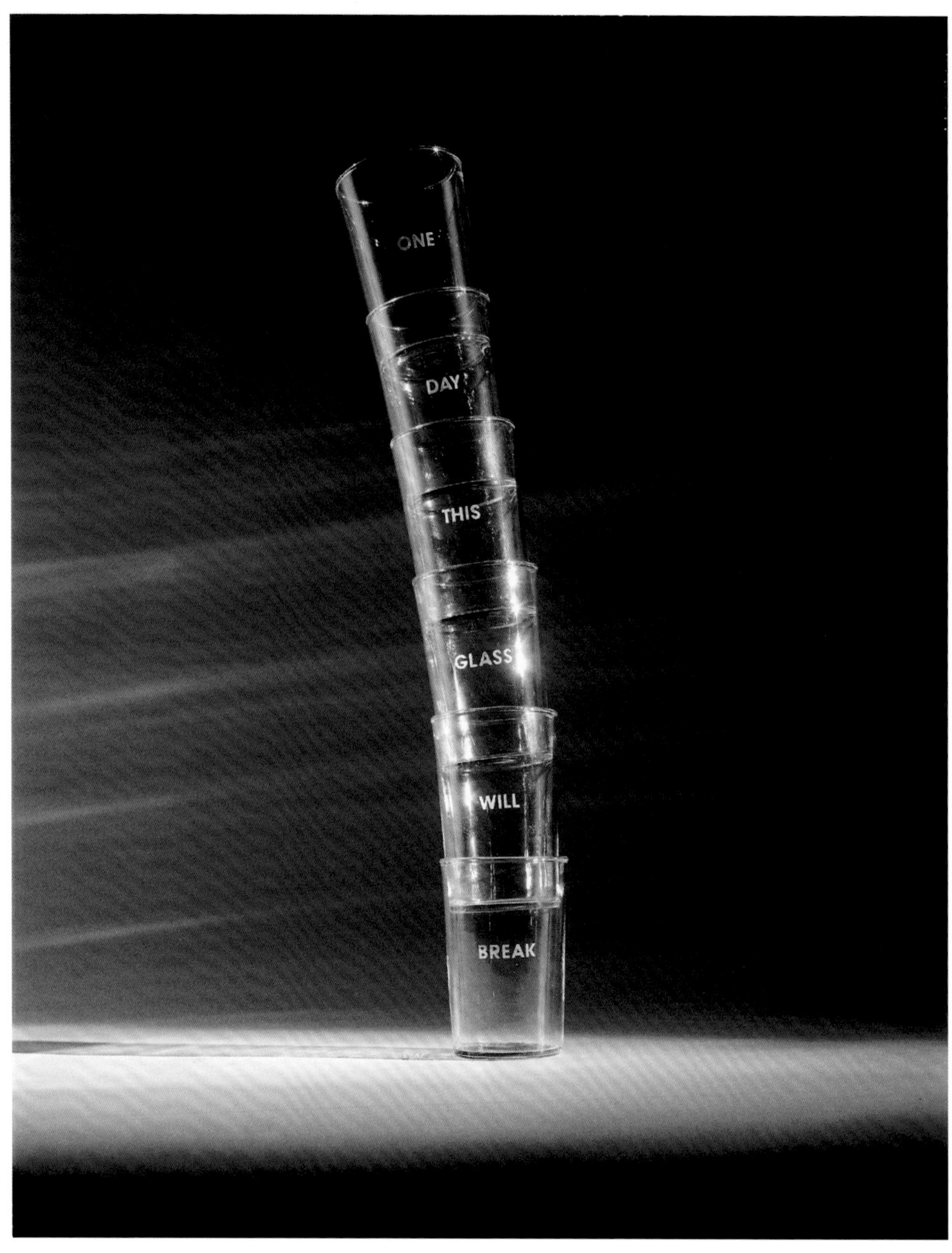

One Day This Glass Will Break 1997
Six etched glasses (stacked), 43 × 7.5

universal truth: we all leave traces and we all make creases without thinking. As a kid, I loved seeing those photographic teasers in newspapers asking, 'What is this?'; it'd be a close-up of a match head or something. Any familiar object becomes abstract when seen through a microscope. For some reason that was for me so compelling.

D When you read the early books on photography they're talking about automatism and efficiency and standardisation, but now what seems to appeal to us about early photography is its complete failure to do all of that! It hadn't yet been industrialised, perfected – so all of those things about chance that you're interested in are right there at the beginning of photography, though for the pioneers those are the obstacles to overcome.

C I loved it when it was in that stage. When things get too slick and over-produced – the Robert Mapplethorpes and all that – I lose interest somehow.

One of the things I did love about making the Fox Talbot-inspired prints was using glass as a material. I'd made a sculpture in 1997 called *One Day This Glass Will Break*, which was a stack of glass tumblers engraved with the words of the title. They had to be stacked at a certain height to read the mantra, but when you did they became much more likely to fall over. It's like the human condition: we're all fragile, we're all going to die. Things with time become increasingly precarious, and at some point, they break.

Revisiting the idea in the recent prints was so enjoyable – laying the glasses down horizontally on the plate rather than vertically, you could achieve a much higher stack (p. 29). By shining UV lights through them you could capture a sense of precipitousness despite

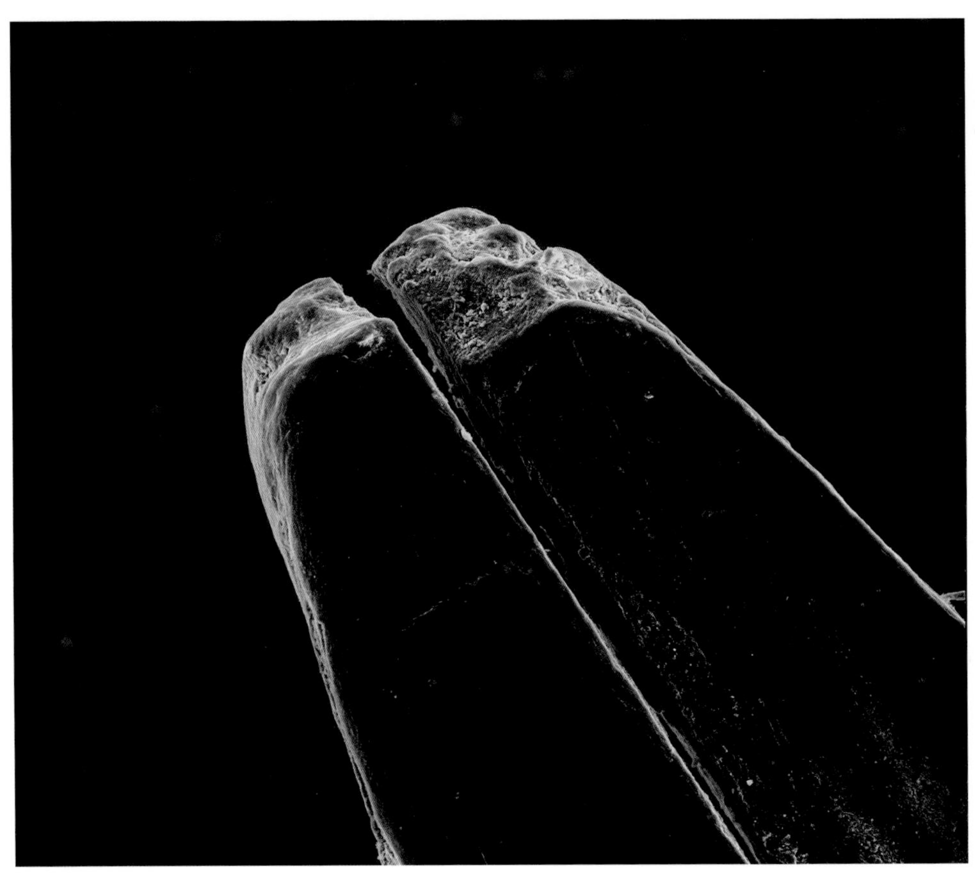

Brontëan Abstract (Emily Brontë's Pen Nib) 2006
Silver gelatin print of a scanning electron microscope image
44.5 × 49.5

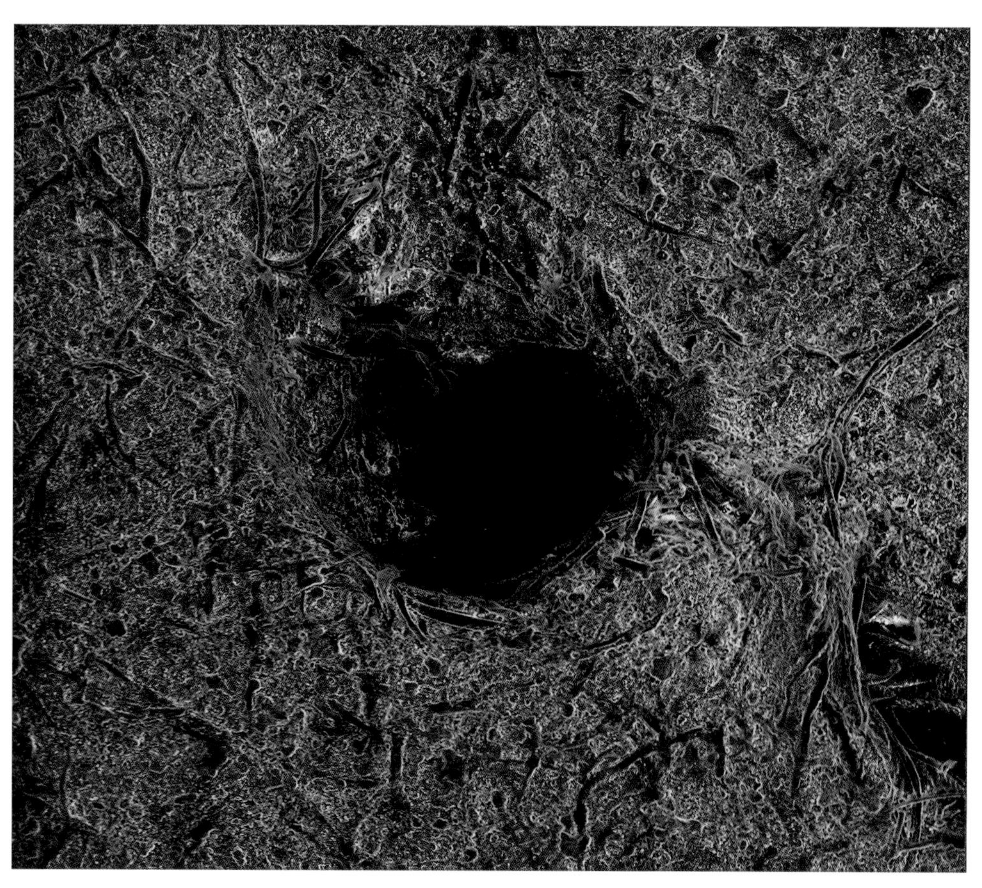

Brontëan Abstract (Pinhole Made by Charlotte Brontë) 2006
Silver gelatin print of a scanning electron microscope image
27.5 × 40.7

the fact they're safely recumbent (pp. 29, 31). A lot of my prints show a moment in transition, like a jug of ice being spilled, then gradually melting.

In making the prints you record a moment but you also need a five-minute exposure to etch the plate. I made a photogravure of a spent theatre light bulb and titled it *An Idea* (p. 33), and then I smashed the same light bulb on different plate a few minutes later, exposed it, and called it *A Premeditated Act of Violence* (p. 35). It was great being able to chase these thoughts through print as quickly as they were occurring to me. Pete Kosowicz – the master printer who runs Thumbprint – and I were like children playing. I said, 'What happens if we put a load of sugar cubes and some ants on this plate? Let's capture the tracks of ants scurrying about.' (We haven't got around to realising that idea yet.) It's about recording something durational, compressing time. I always loved Hiroshi Sugimoto's photographs of cinema screens where the aperture is open for the entire length of the film. It's such a beautiful thing that he's captured the light of every frame that falls on the big screen which in turn illuminates its surroundings. And when photographing the stars you're capturing light that was emitted many light years before. Now there is even the possibility of photographing the beginnings of the universe…

D I think photography is still with us, unlike a lot of other nineteenth-century innovations, because so much is still possible with it. As if we haven't quite got our heads around the implications of what it could do. Here we are in 2017 and my phone is in front of me – you might think, 'Well, that's the latest technology,' but Fox Talbot would recognise it. He'd see that there's a little black box in there that takes photos… it's staggering that we've not left that behind, really.

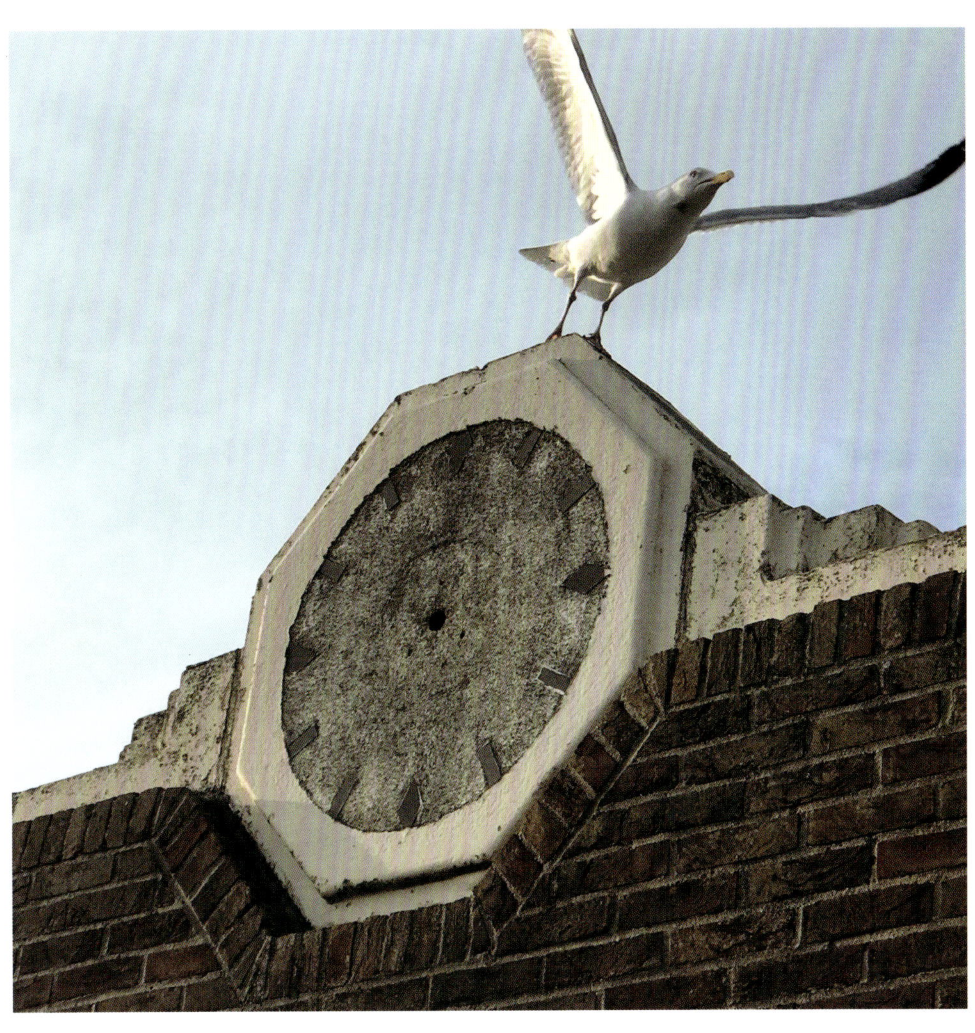

Time Flies 2018
This and all images to p. 73 are photographs taken by Cornelia Parker

C My phone has now replaced my sketchbook.

D And do you take a lot of photographs in your working process, just as notation?

C Oh, all the time. Now, with Instagram, you can juxtapose a caption with an image and convey an idea spontaneously in seconds. Posting images on Instagram is new to me: I had to do some social media in my role as Official Election Artist in 2017, and Instagram was the lesser evil. It meant every image I posted could be read with a political slant. I found myself photographing the right- (*Sun*) and left-wing (*Mirror*) newspapers sitting side by side in my local newsagent every day. Everything was colour-coded: blue things were Tory, red Labour, etc. I even posted images of the evening TV news, some of the news items were just too hard to resist (*Dotards*, p. 68). Instagram is strange in terms of people 'liking' an image, as I was often posting unpalatable things, the homeless (p. 61), Ukip thugs, *Daily Mail* headlines…

Before Instagram I used to take hundreds of photos and laboriously email them to friends. Richard Wentworth is the ultimate antecedent of Instagram with his *Making Do and Getting By* series. He emails images to people incessantly – cryptic, and tailored to the person in mind. Sometimes, if you are lucky, he might even drop something through your letterbox in the middle of the night.

D Through my twenties I used to shoot two or three 35mm films, get prints from the lab, and literally post the photos. Friends have several hundred of these. So, when people started talking about 'posting' images in the social media sense, I thought, 'Oh this is just an extension of that kind of sharing.'

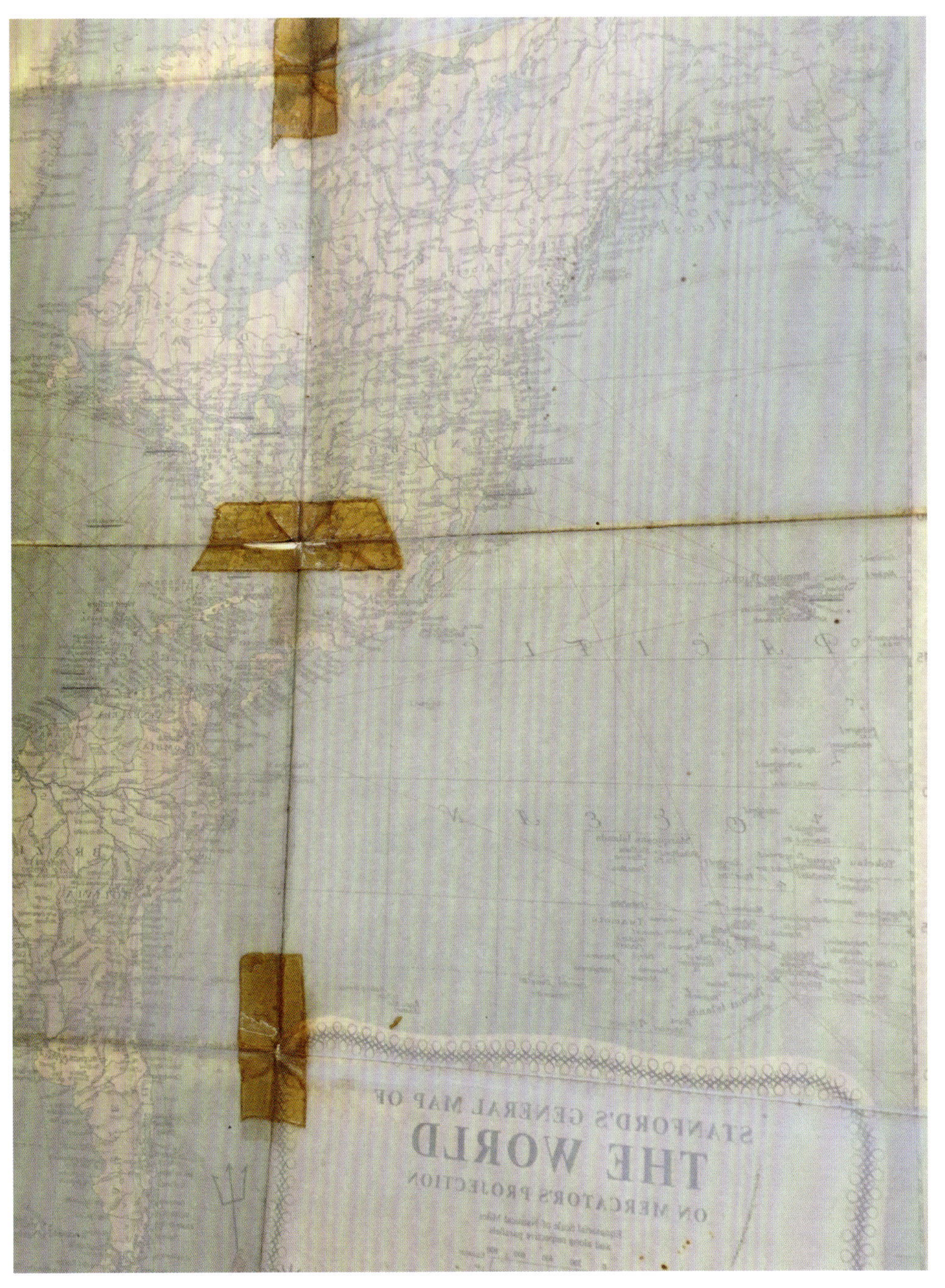

World Coming Apart at the Seams 2017

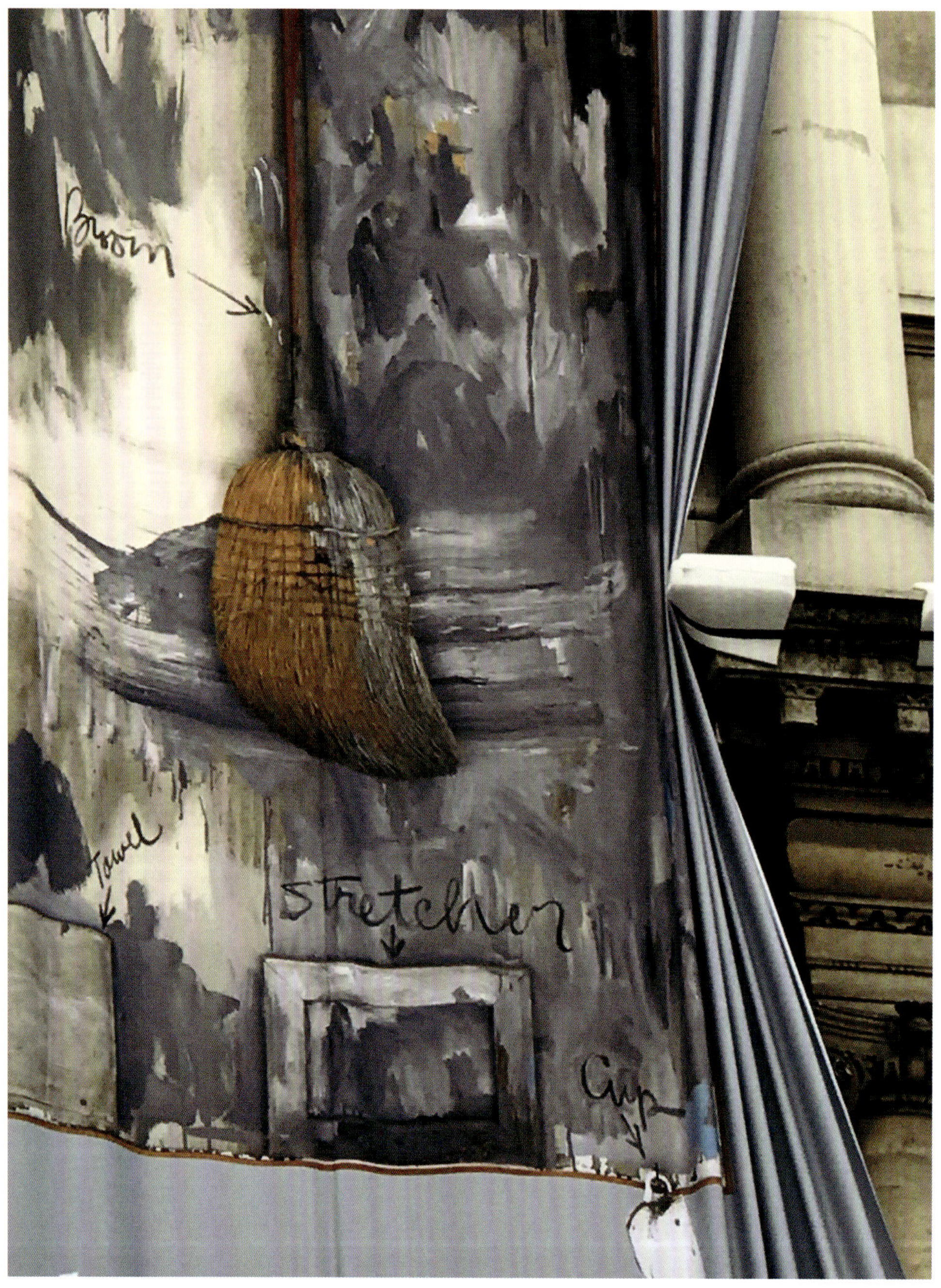
Broom
Towel
Stretcher
Cup

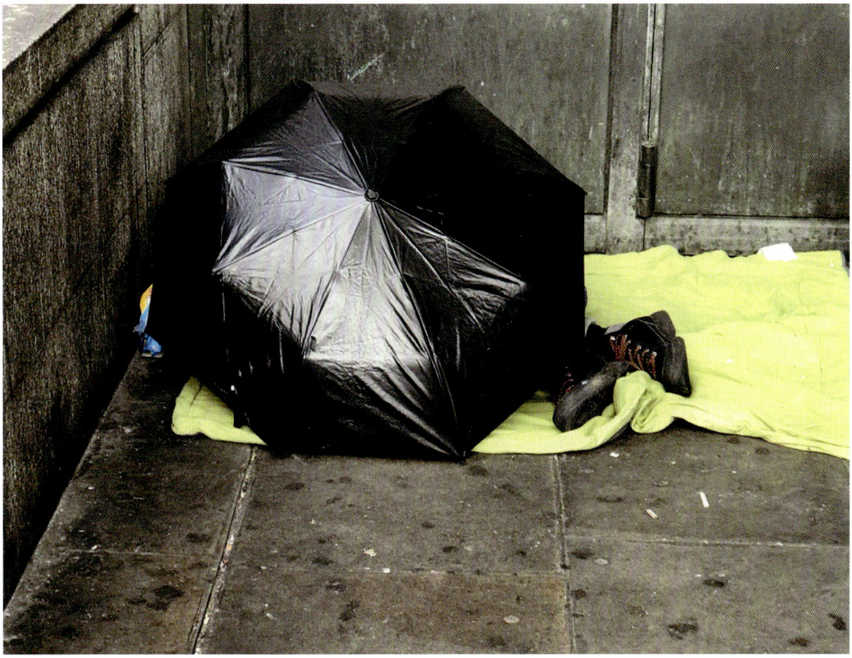

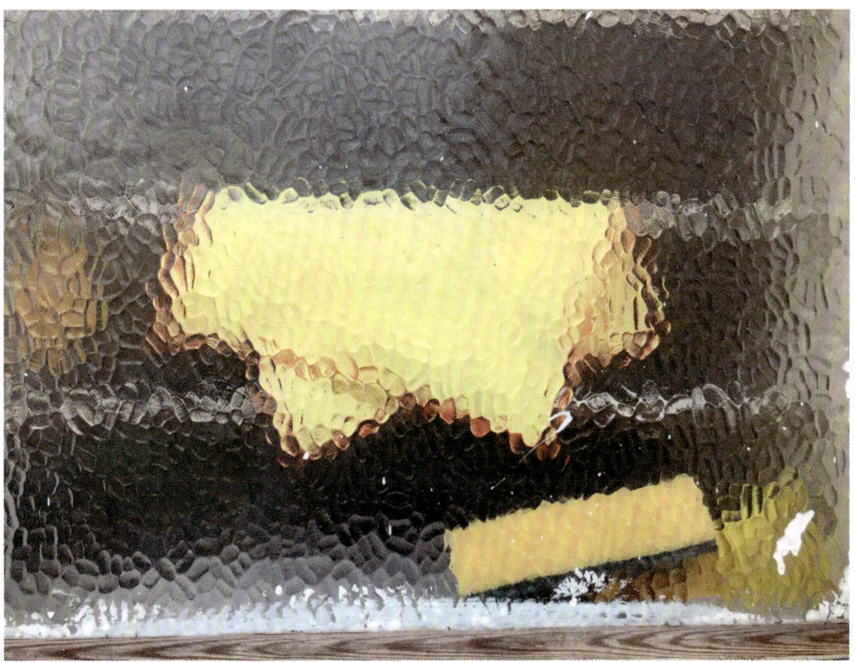

top: **Westminster** 2018
bottom: **Duster** 2018

Sharing is an important part of your work, too. Clearly you have your own obsessions, but what comes across is a kind of wonder – not the conveying of your subjectivity. I just feel I'm being shown something and asked to engage with a phenomenon of the world.

C I like photographing found photos whenever they crop up in my travels. There is a cracked ceramic plaque on top of the Mount of Olives that bears a photographic image showing the view of Jerusalem. It is all smashed up with bits of chewing gum stuck on it. It seems to reflect all the conflict that has beset the city over the centuries (p. 65). *Weight on Their Shoulders*, for example, features a 4lb weight sitting on a pile of vintage photographs in Bermondsey antiques market, to stop them flying away. The circular weight looks like it is bearing down on the image of some innocent pre-war boys, mud-larking on the banks of the Thames, an ominous omen perhaps of horrors to come (p. 63). A poster of a gigantic guinea pig captured outside a pet store looks like a genetic experiment gone wrong (p. 64). A banner advertising the Jasper Johns exhibition at the Royal Academy, snagged on a pediment becomes *Impediment* (p. 60).

I'm mining ordinary everyday objects to unleash catalysts for thought, and hopefully there's some space there for others to run with it too. That's what I hope people pick up from the work. They don't have to take it literally or anything, although it is very literal! [laughs]

D But often the very literal is itself a complete release for people.

C You don't have to worry about working out what the meaning is.

D It's an occasion.

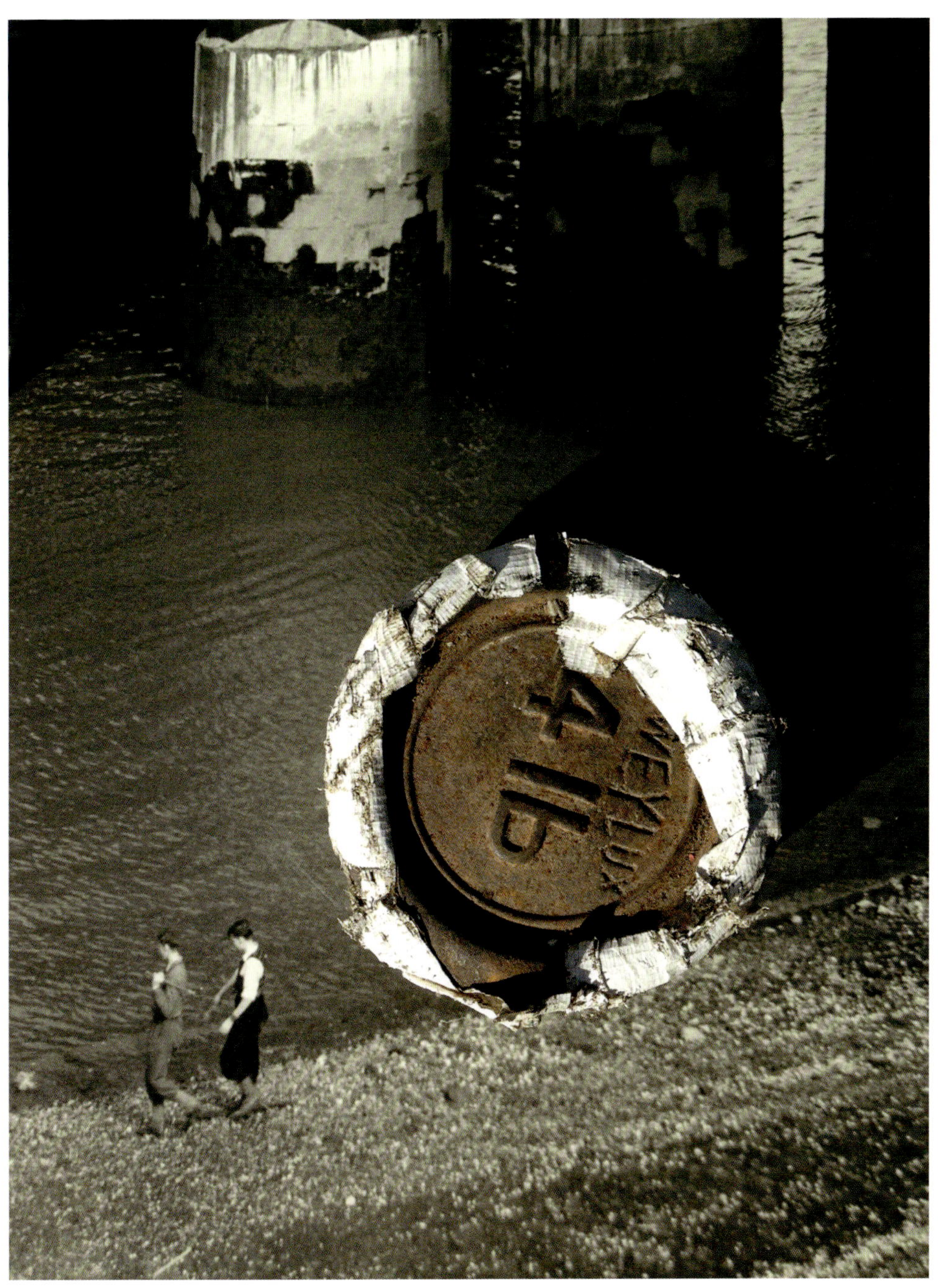

Weight on Their Shoulders 2018

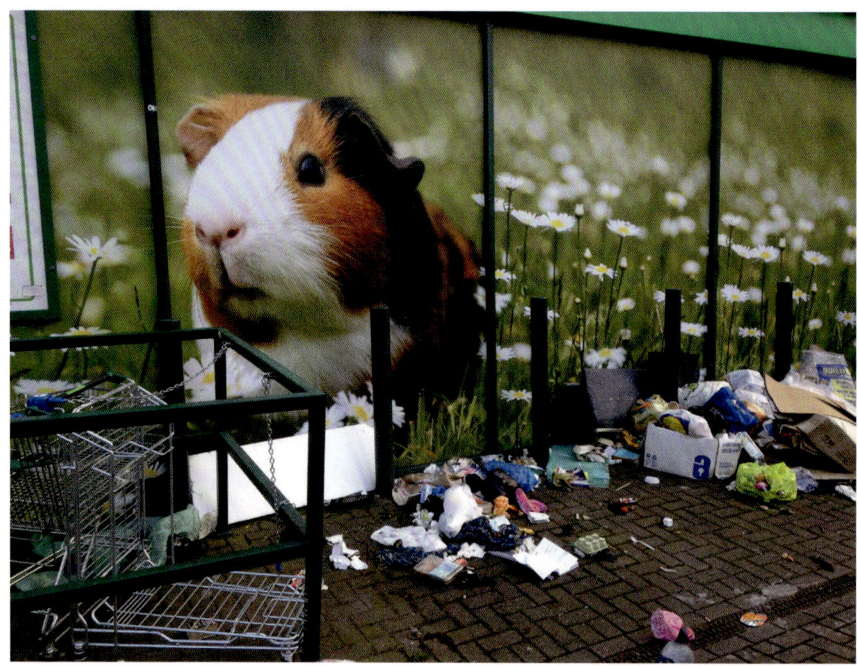

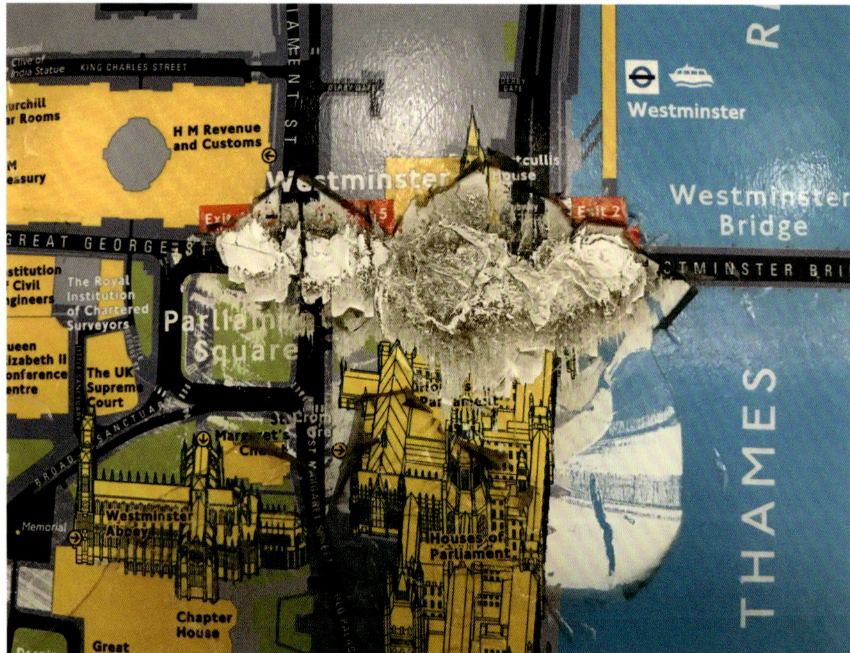

top: **The Future** 2017
bottom: **Westminster** 2017

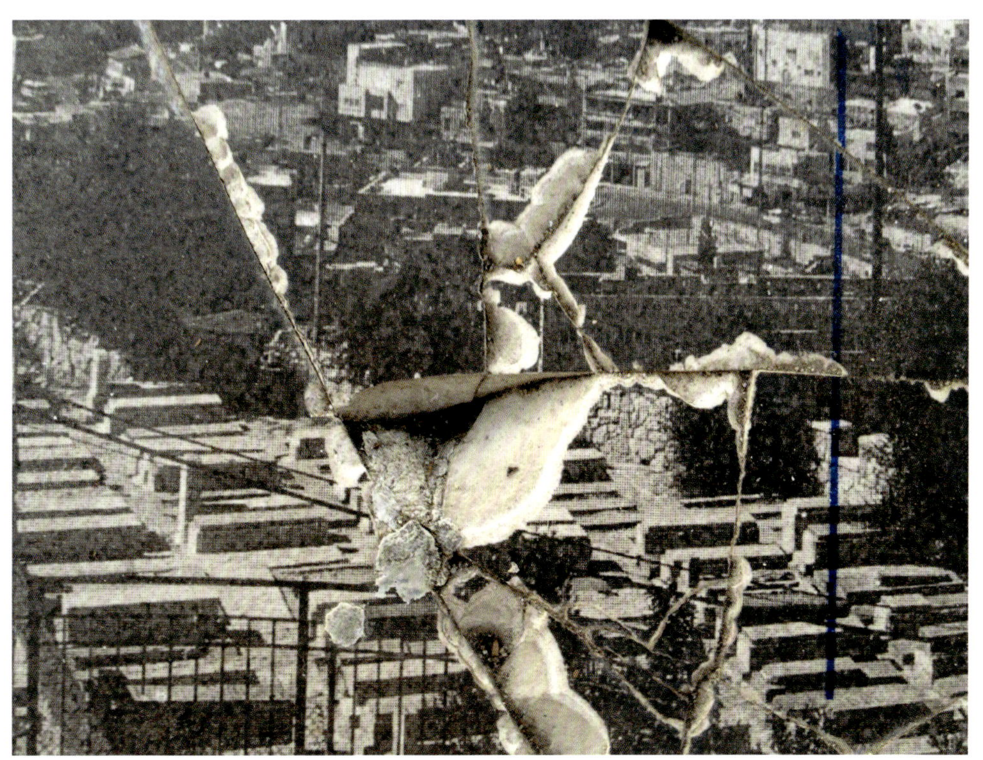

Broken View (Mount of Olives, Jerusalem) 2012

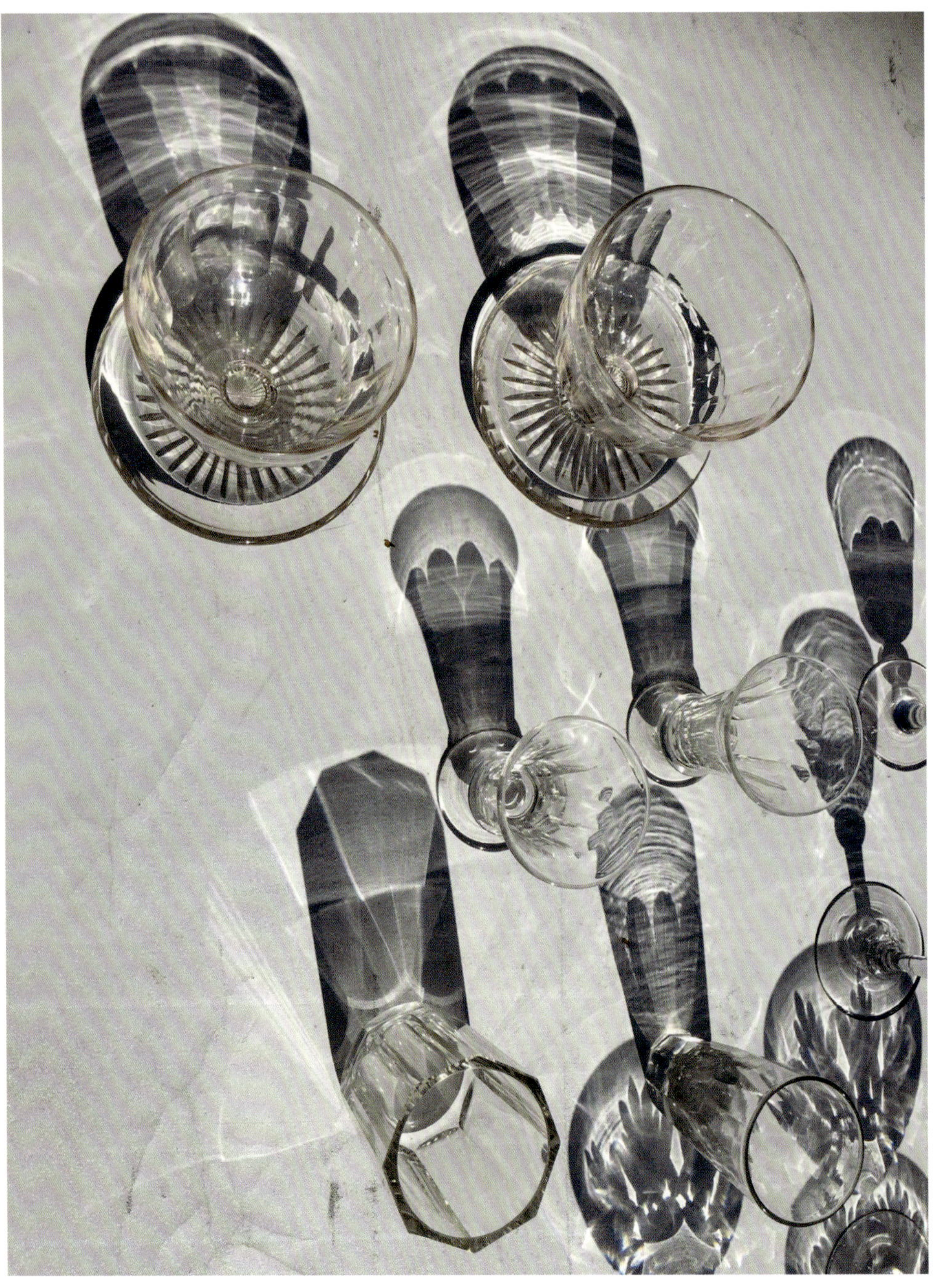

Sun and Glass 2018

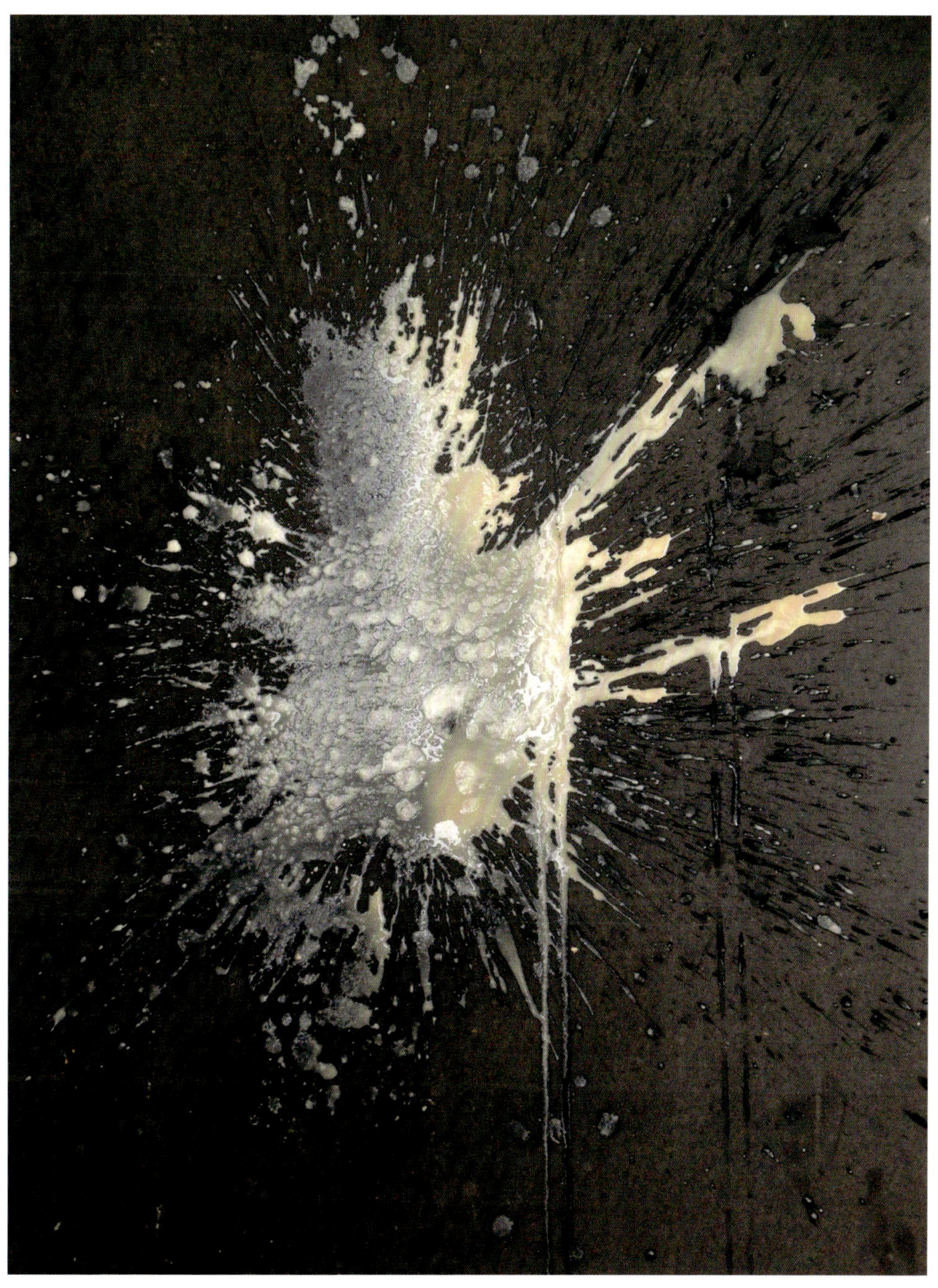

Incident (Brussels) 2017

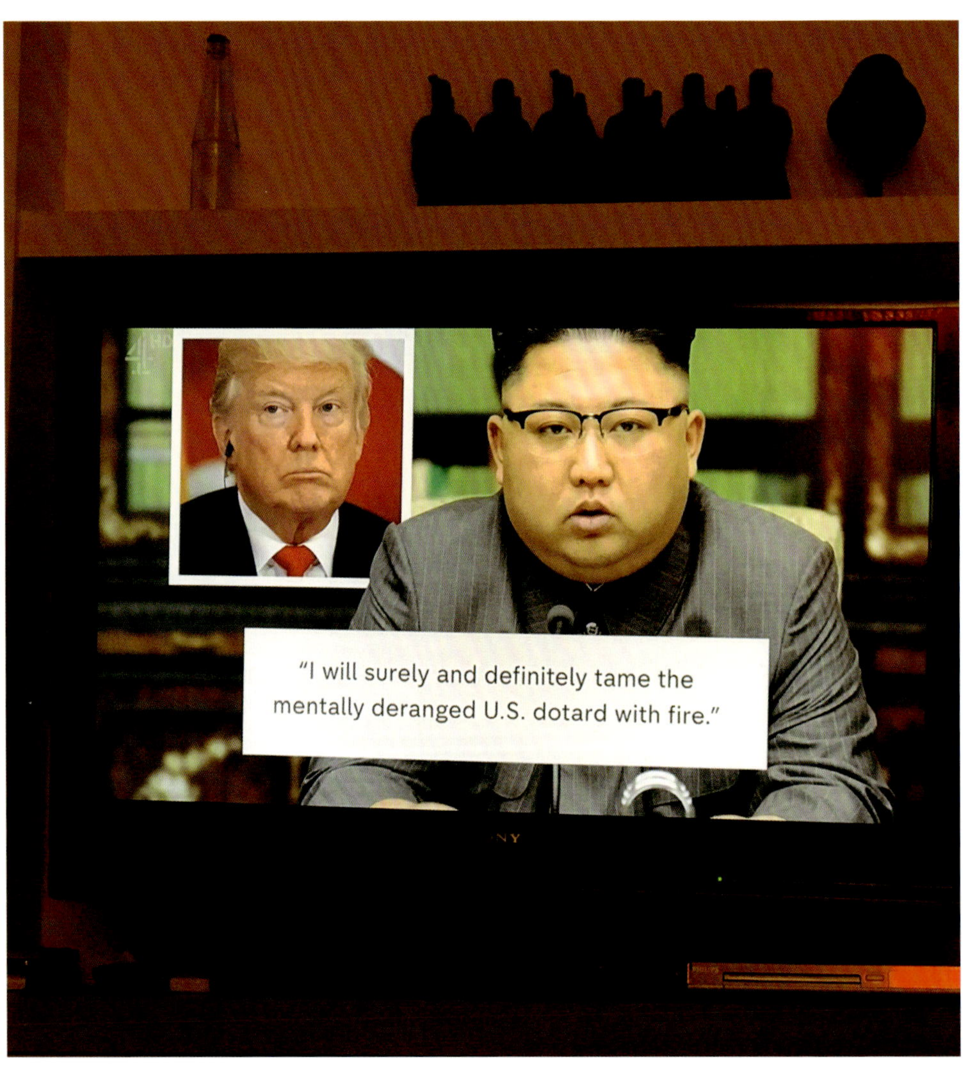

Dotards 2017

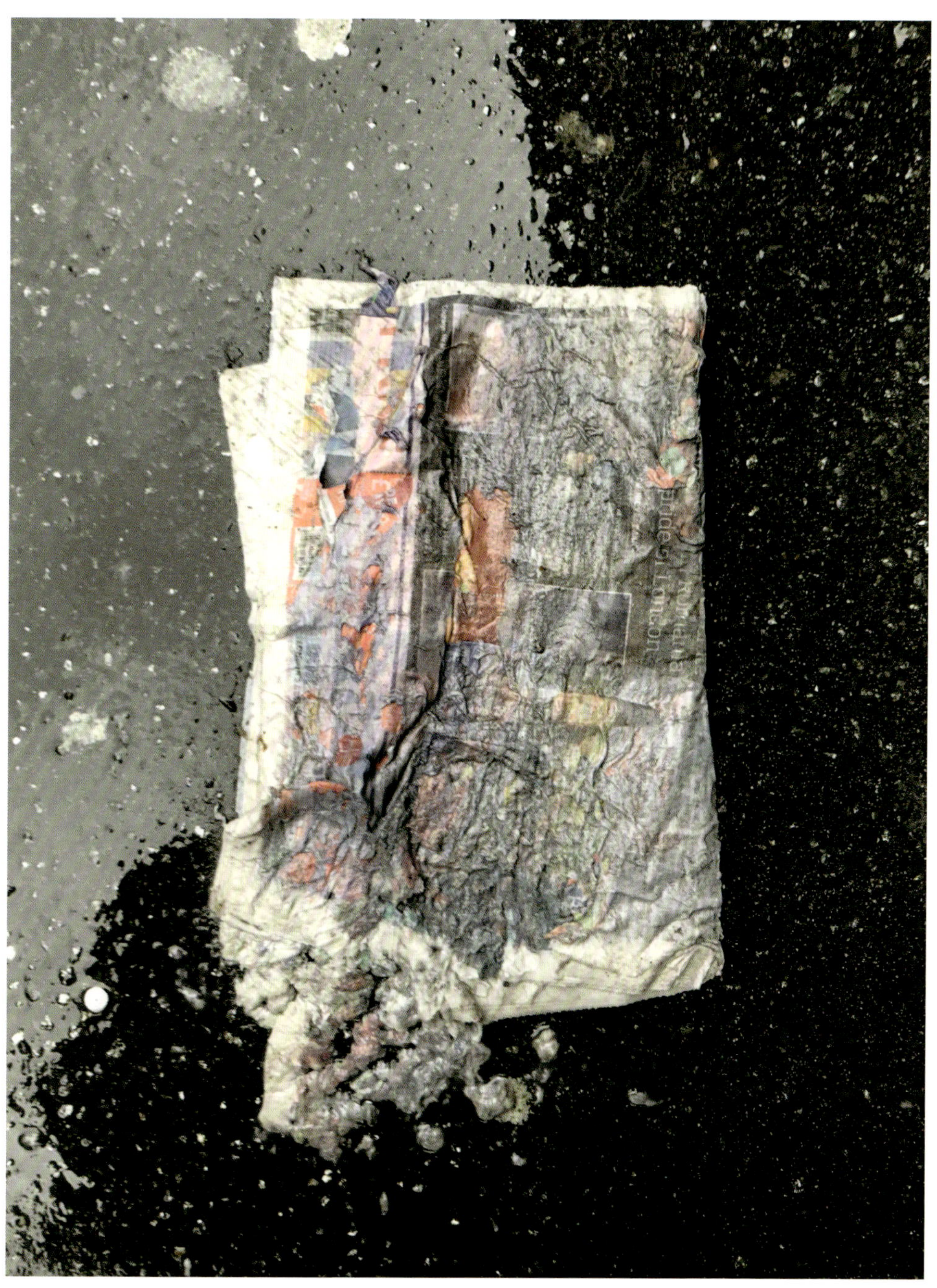

Yesterday's News 2017

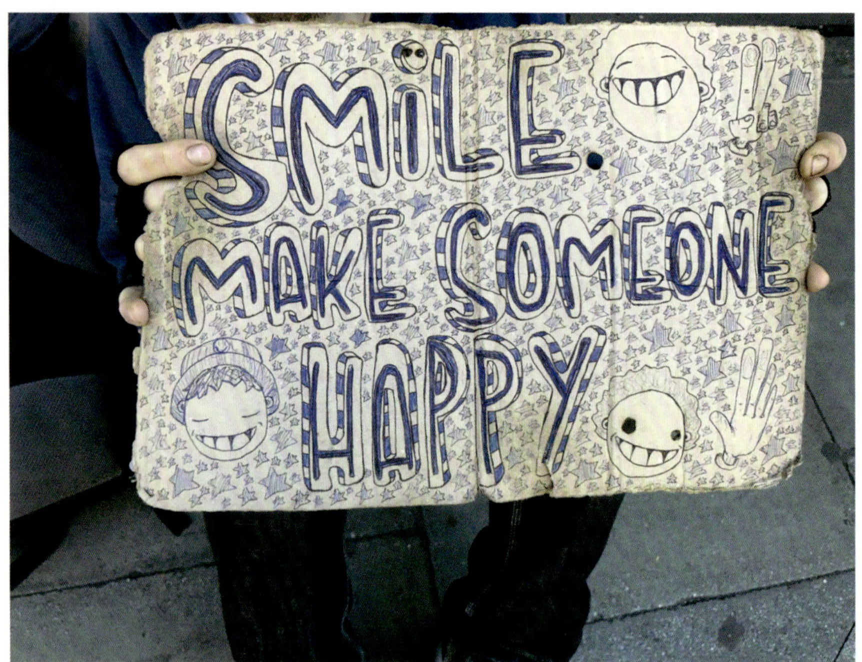

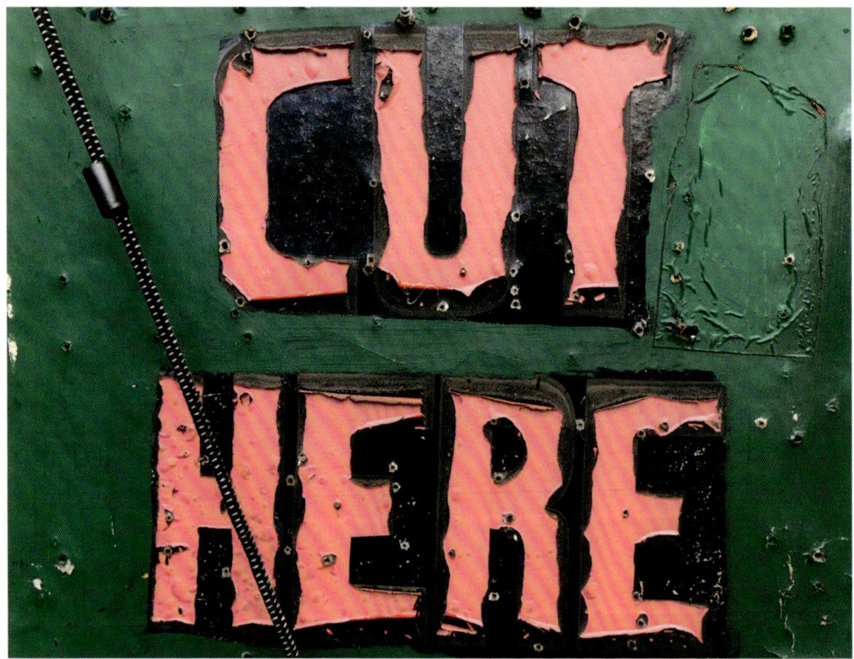

top: **Smile** 2017
bottom: **Cut Here** 2017

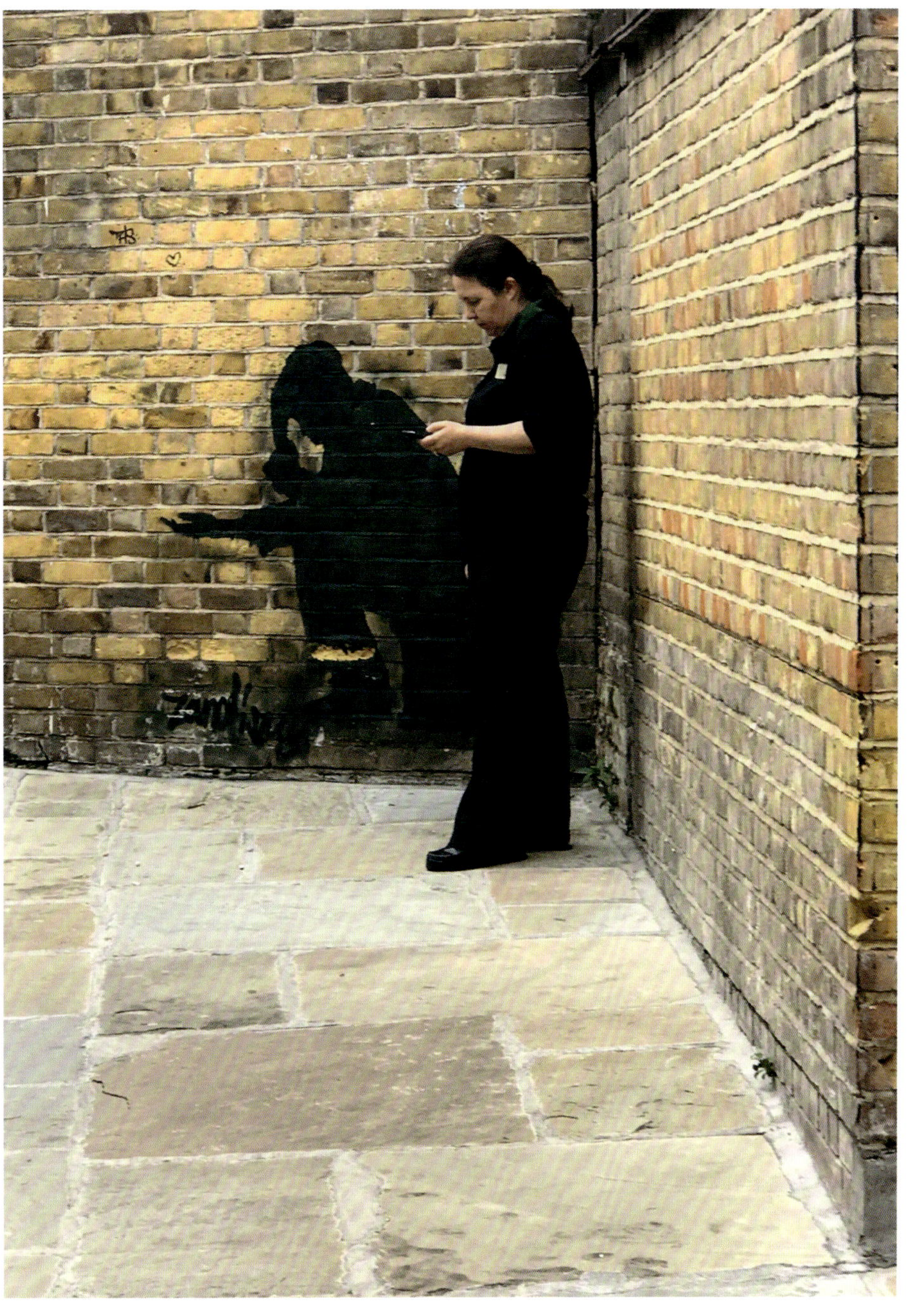

Hands Out 2017

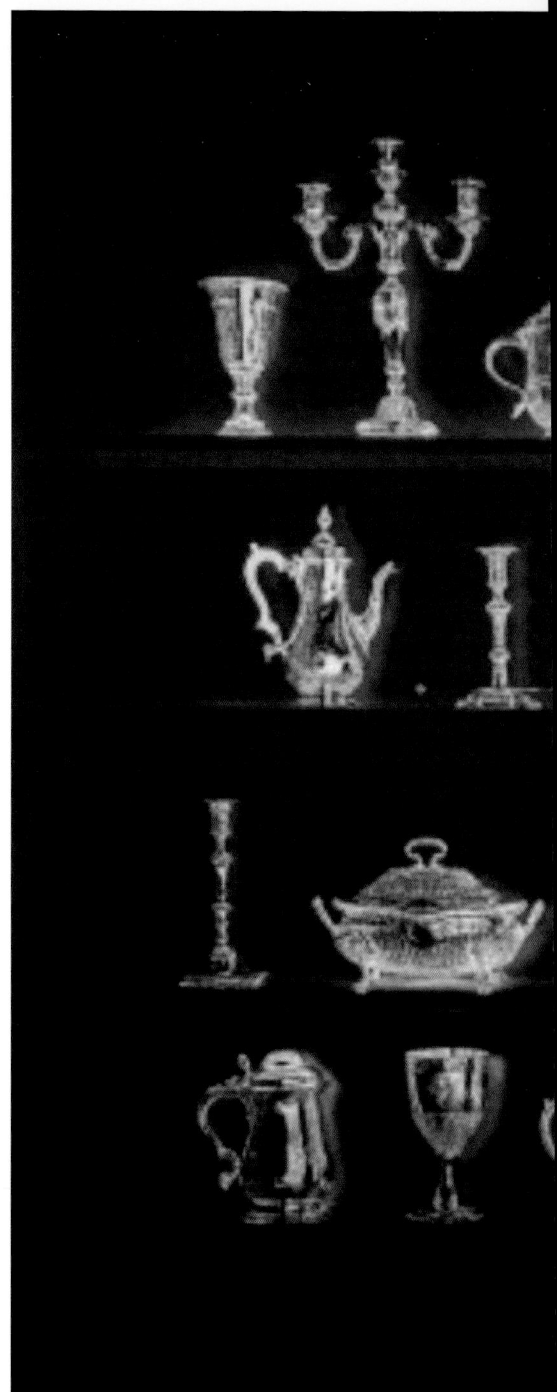

Thirty Pieces of Silver Minus One 2017
Wool, silk, metal thread
247 × 295.5 × 1

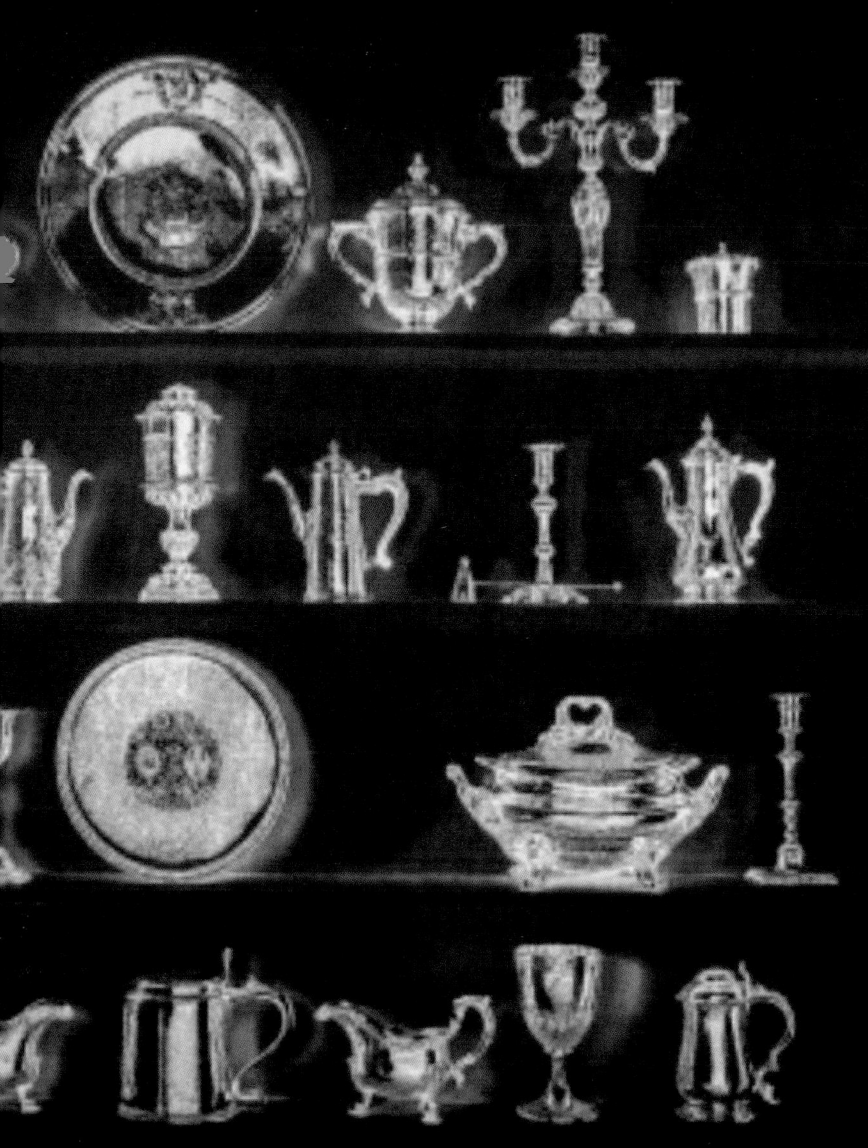

C. An occasion, yes – like squashing a brass band for *Perpetual Canon*; the wind instruments might have been robbed of their breath but they have been resurrected by being suspended, appearing as *trompe l'oeil* versions of their former selves. Everyone can see the damage; the process is laid bare. By flattening objects they occupy only a sliver of the space they once did (a state that Duchamp would call *inframince*), but the sound lost to them is replaced by the drama of their cacophonous display (pp. 84–87).

--

D Your titles are super-careful, aren't they? You're as playful with words as you are with objects or processes. Somewhere between Duchamp and Beckett.

C Perhaps I'm a Dadaist at heart. Duchamp is funny; precious and yet not precious. He's very considered and sometimes wilfully obscure, but for me it doesn't impede my enjoyment of the work.

D He understood so much about the fact that once you get into the twentieth century, the distance between the artwork and its reproduction begins to collapse – and his work has the same sort of relation to reproduction as yours has. I've been going through your catalogues, and there are pieces I haven't seen – I only know them as photographs. And of course, if I saw them as objects, they would have other qualities. But there's something about the way your work translates into photographic reproduction that I'm interested in. I'm also interested in scale of reproduction. If one is painting or making a sculptural work then scale and materiality are integral to what you're doing. But when you make a photographic image, unless it's a photogram or you're spilling something directly across the photogravure plate, you can blow it up. It's not like a painter paints their painting and then decides how big it's going to be. There's something about photography not having an integral scale, not having an integral relation to material.

C Yes, though I also like things that do hold their scale. I made a piece called *Different Dirt*, for which I scanned objects I'd bought on eBay that had been dug up by a metal detector on opposite sides of the Atlantic. On eBay, you see all these photos made by the sellers formally laying out their finds, not unlike Fox Talbot. I wanted to relocate, to re-bury these found objects in a different location, on another continent. Those dug up in Britain, like Roman coins, for example, I had buried in Athens, Georgia – in a bit of reverse archaeology, things that were lost and then found were lost again. I scanned the objects actual size with the day's newspaper held high up above so it looked very dark. The viewer gets the text from the eBay ad, the scan, and a caption saying, 'Dug up in Cheshire and buried in Athens, Georgia'.

D Photographs or traces of something in transit.

C The objects don't look fixed like they do in the advert – instead they appear to be in free fall. The scanned image simply records their time above ground, just before they get buried again.

D You mention objects for sale on eBay looking like Fox Talbot's shelves arranged either with books or glassware or china. I'm always struck by how much of what the early pioneers covered is so contemporary. I teach a course on the history of photography to undergraduates at the University of Westminster, and it's so easy to make connections between what all of those pioneers were doing and what happens now. A photographer still faces the same practical problem: how do you show objects?

METAL DETECTOR FINDS-lead indian & soldiers

Item # 312352357

Found, using a metal detector, these 4 lead, I think, figures. There is an Indian, stands 3 1/3" tall. Is missing his hand, and some of his paint. He is carring a yellow and blue shield. There is a soldier with a gun, 2 3/4" tall. He is missing some paint and looks like some of his platform. A wounded Japanese soldier, 2 3/4" tall, with his arm in a sling and a bandage around his head. Looks like he is missing part of his leg and a foot. He is also missing some paint. There is another soldier, 2" tall. I don't know what he is, in a red and blue uniform. Has a very small head with some sort of thing from his hat. He is carring a gun, and has a yellow pack on his back. There is a soldier laying down with some kind of large gun. Poor guy is missing his head. There is a small hard plastic soldier 1 3/4" tall saluting. He is just dirty.

UNEARTHED IN NORTH CAROLINA, USA
REBURIED IN BATTLE, NEAR HASTINGS, ENGLAND 2003

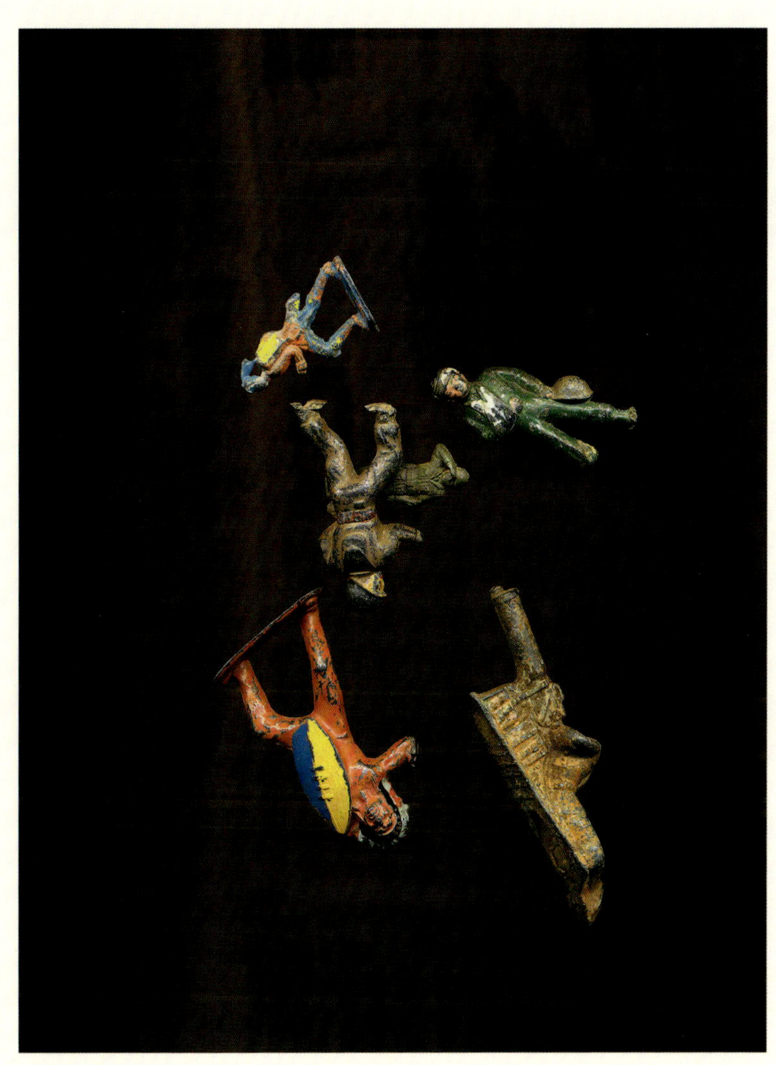

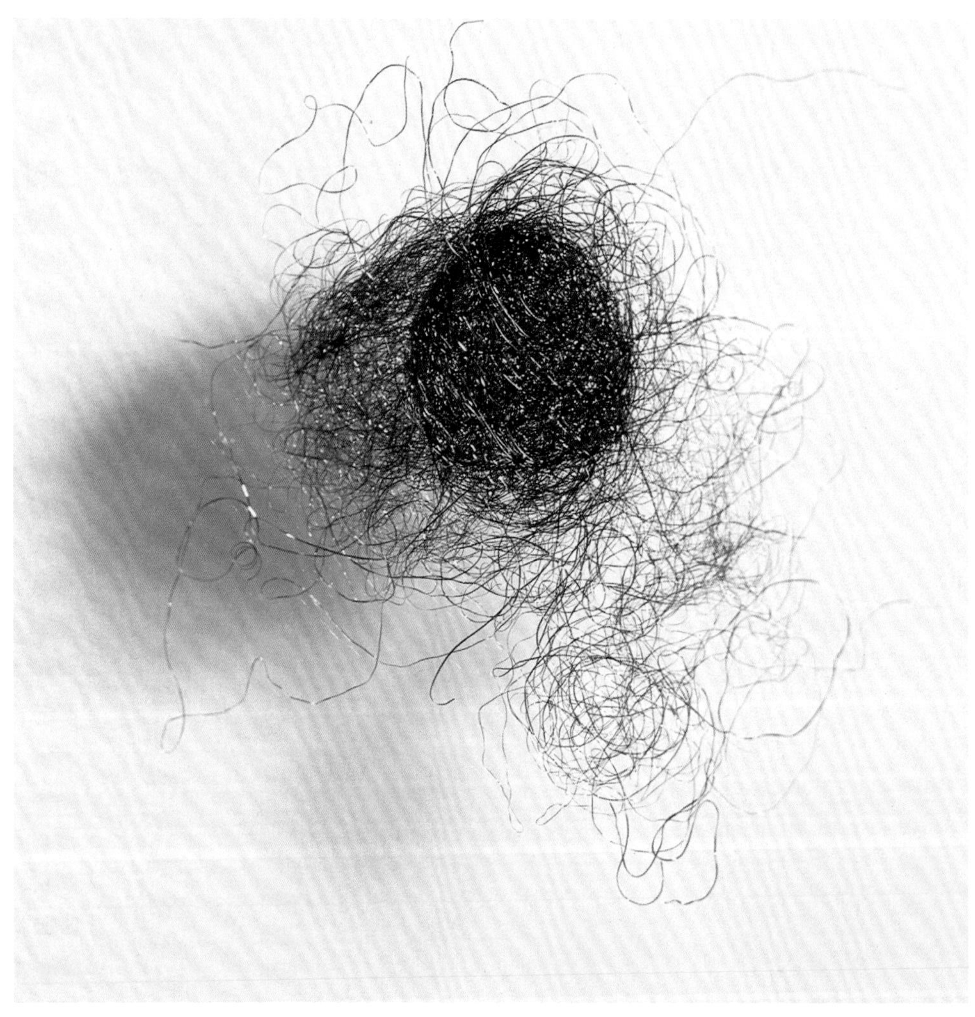

The Negatives of Sound 1996 (detail)
Black lacquer residue from cutting the grooves when mastering records, 63 × 63, framed
With thanks to Abbey Road Studios

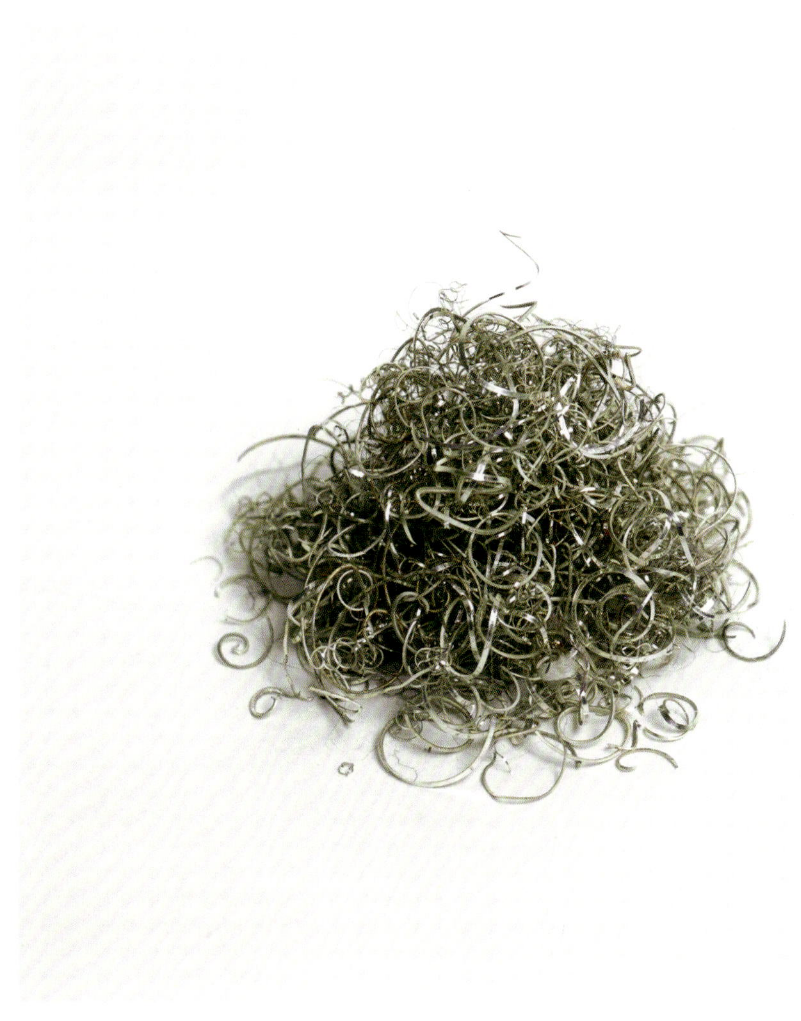

The Negative of Words 1996
Silver residue accumulated from engraving words by hand
10.5 × 10.5 × 7.8

C Or how do you catalogue them? My Ivory Press book titled *Verso* consists of 80 photographs of the flipside of cards displaying buttons from a museum's collection. All the buttons have been sewn onto the cards in ordered grids or regimented patterns, but their undersides reveal the individuality of the stitcher and their own particular logic of getting a thread from A to B (pp. 81–82). *Verso* harks back to *Room for Margins* (1998) where I exhibited Turner's canvas liners, the backs of his paintings, as works in their own right. I've made several pieces exploring ideas of the inverse and the negative. *The Negative of Words* is a little pile of metal shavings excavated by a silversmith when he was engraving letters into silver by hand. *The Negative of Sound* is made from the lacquer swarf made when cutting the original groove when mastering records at Abbey Road Studios (pp. 78, 79).

D Coming back to this interest in cataloguing… Fox Talbot's *Articles of Glass*, with its grid-like pattern, looks like it could have been made at any time really.

C I've just made a tapestry for Trinity Hall in Cambridge, to replace one that went missing around Oliver Cromwell's time. It was donated by Doctor Eden, Master of the College, who as a parliamentarian managed to save the silver belonging to the college from confiscation by parliamentarians. They gave me an open brief so I made a piece based on Fox Talbot and his shelves. Fox Talbot was at Trinity College next door, but he'd been known to frequent the dining hall where this piece is displayed. The tapestry depicts 30 pieces of the college silver dating back to the 1100s. Trinity Hall allowed me to melt one of the objects down and it's been made into wire and threaded through the rest of the tapestry. Hence its title, *Thirty Pieces of Silver Minus One*, the ultimate betrayal (pp. 72–73). I made a little film of it being unveiled and posted it on my Instagram.

Image from Cornelia Parker's artist's book, **Verso** (Madrid: Ivory Press, 2017)

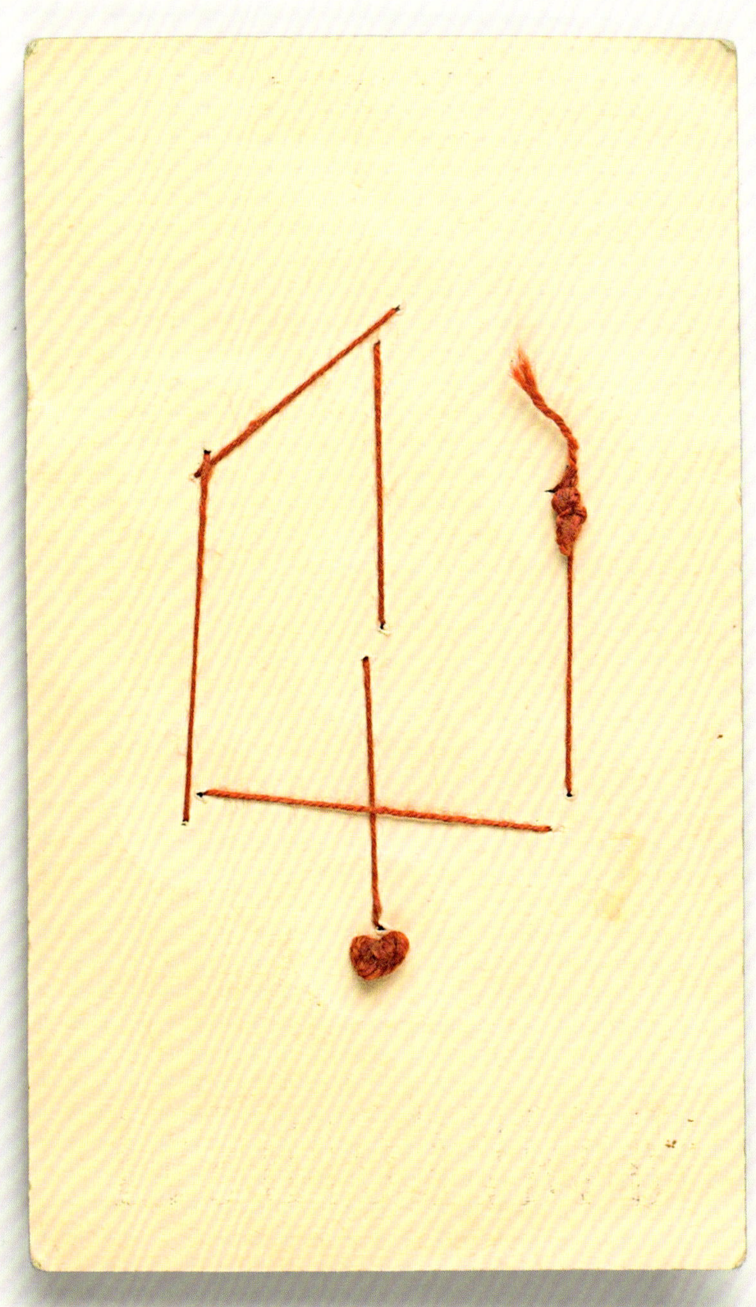

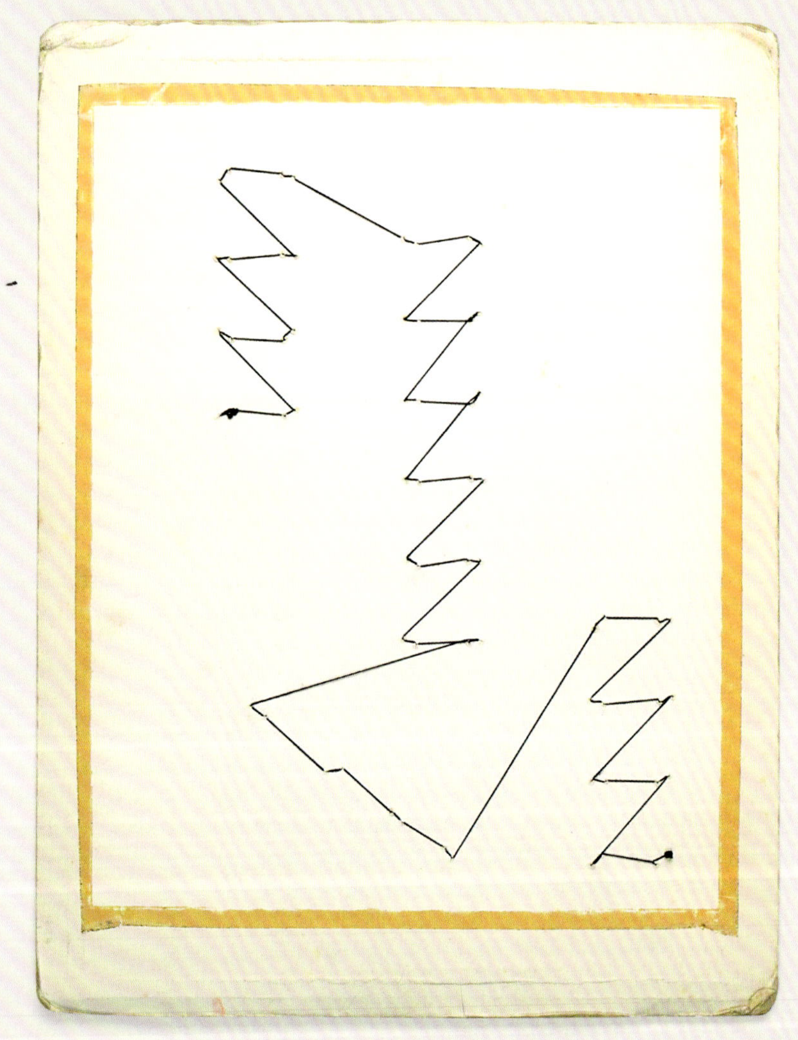

D I love the fact that a Cromwellian tapestry inspired a Talbotian response, and we're looking at it on Instagram!

C It's been made on a jacquard loom in Flanders, and is based on a photographic negative of the college silver taken in my studio.

D Do you reflect much on your own work? Because all of it seems of a piece to me. There's clearly a pool of fascinations, such as photography, which for you are kind of timeless. They're part of your artistic universe.

C I like revisiting my own earlier works. Something I made at the age of 25 would be approached differently at the age I am now. My early work shows somebody enthusiastically making broad strokes and then moving swiftly on. Now I want to carefully retrace steps and pick up the fine detail that I wasn't interested in back then. In your twenties you're busy opening cupboard doors and taking out the very first thing you see, and then going into another cupboard, and typically leaving the all doors open. I'm very pleased to hear you think it's all of a piece. Obviously it all comes from me, but it does seem like it takes on every different form that's possible.

D But when you look at the arc of Duchamp's career, it feels like that too. In the space of a decade, he's in a hurry and explores things, such profound things, so quickly that I get the impression even he was startled. But what follows for him is a very careful return to this or that implication of a set of concerns he'd already established for himself. If someone can grasp the work quite quickly, although the implications will take a lifetime to figure out, the viewer often presumes that that artist got to that really quickly. But there's Duchamp the ideas man, and Duchamp the very diligent craftsman. He had to put enormous energy into making things look very easy.

Image from Cornelia Parker's artist's book, **Verso** (Madrid: Ivory Press, 2017)

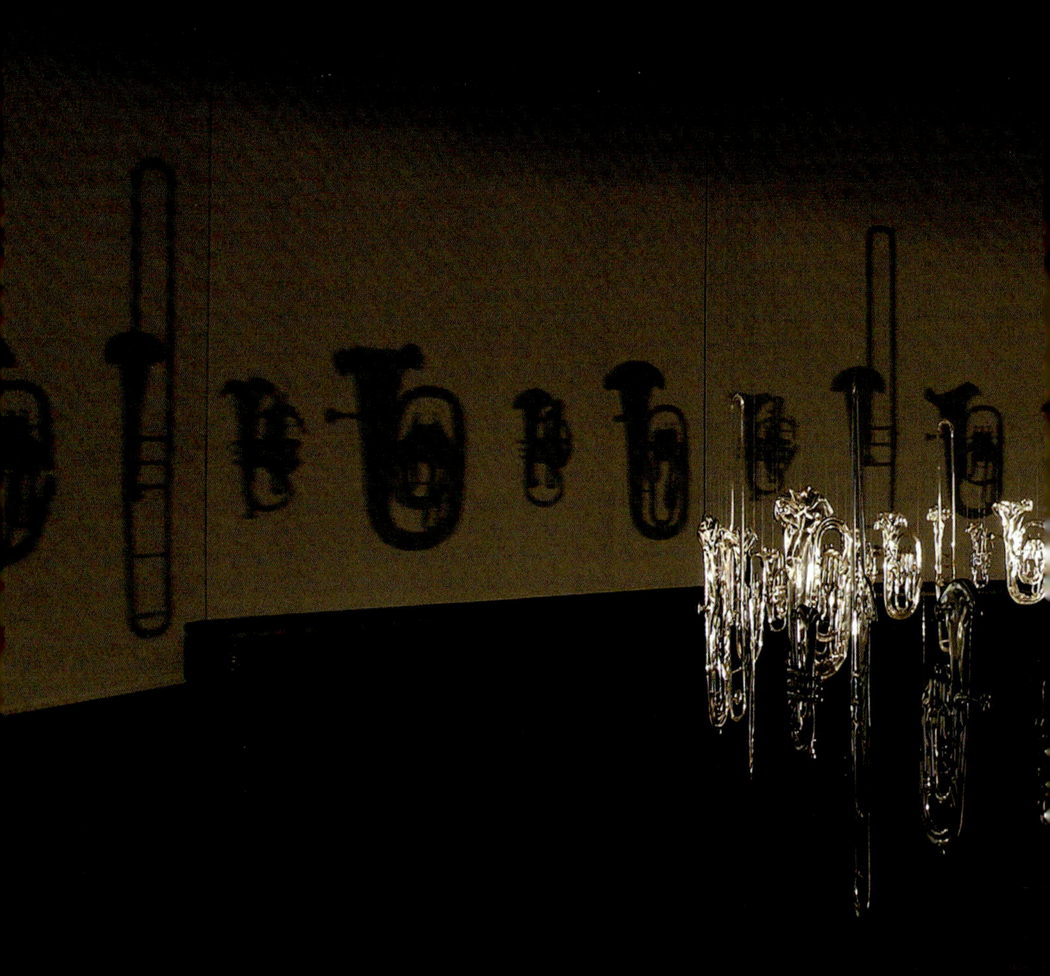

Perpetual Canon 2004
Flattened silver-plated brass-band instruments,
700 × 700

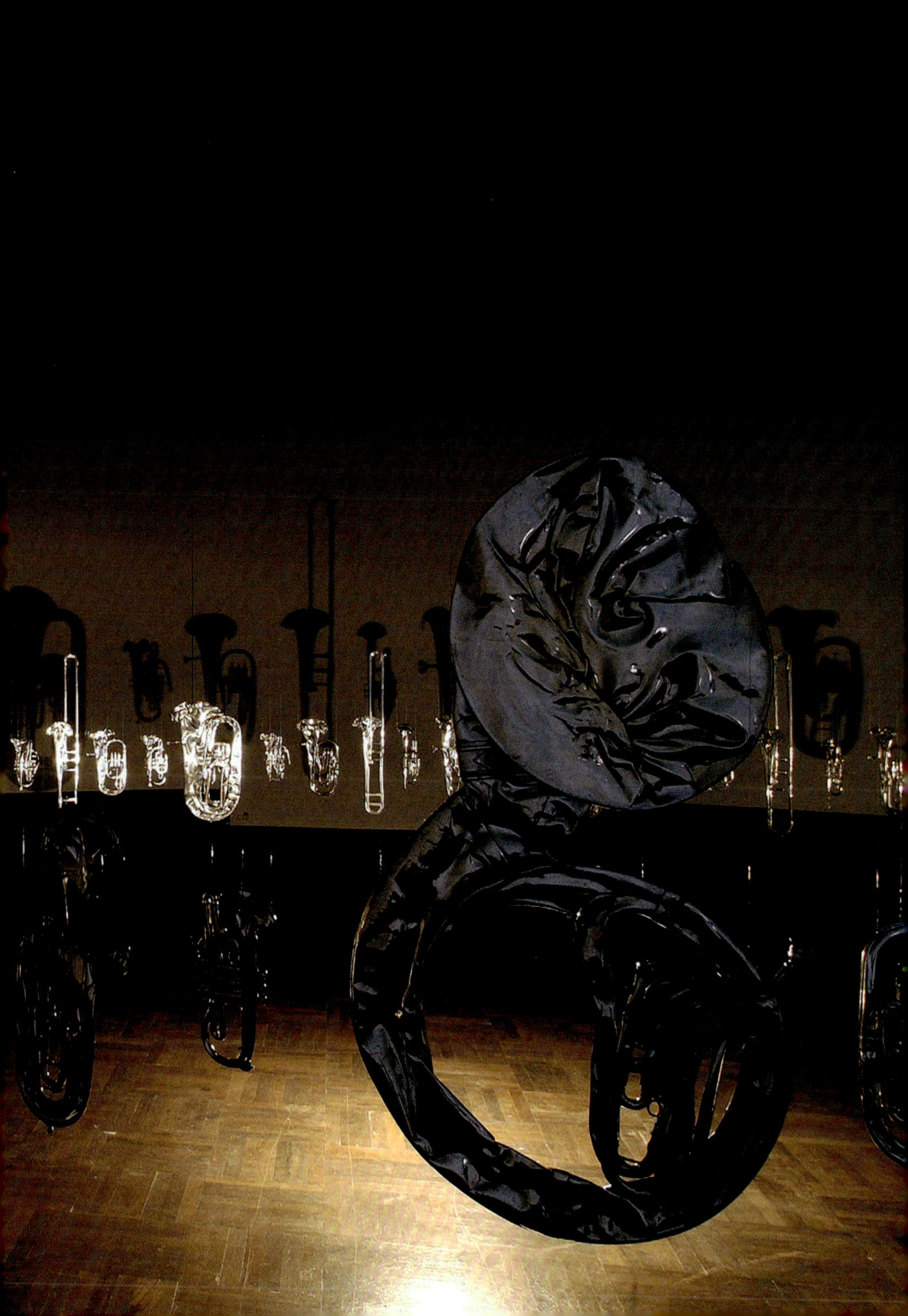

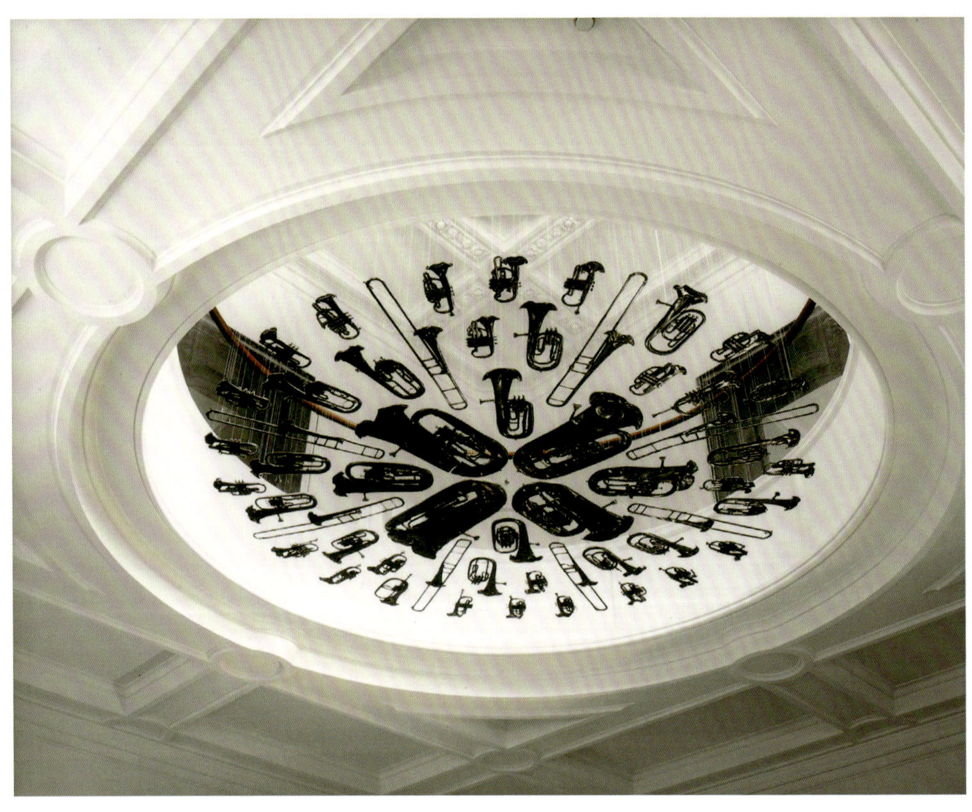

Breathless 2001
Brass musical instruments squashed by a 22-tonne accumulator made for Tower Bridge, London, 500 × 500 × 6
Permanent commission for the Victoria and Albert Museum, London

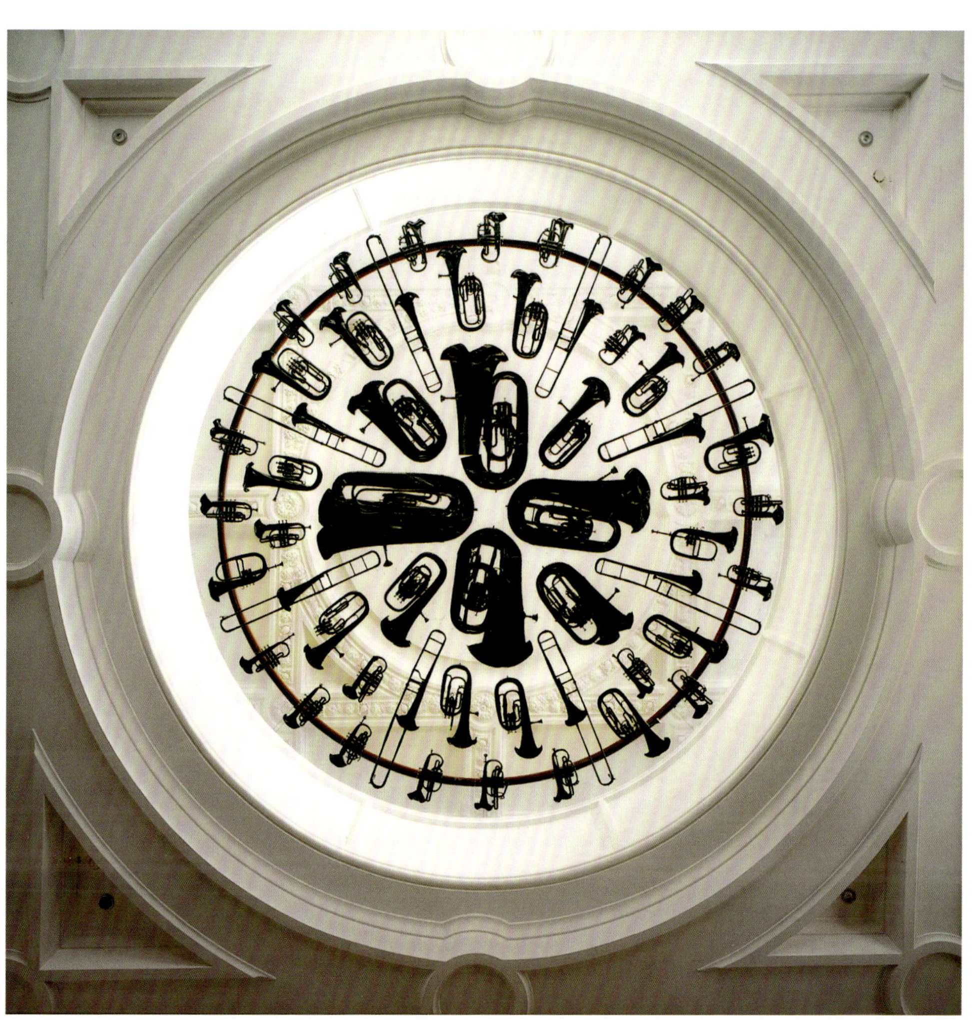

What's the expression? 'It's simple to complicate things but it's complicated to simplify'.

C I like to simplify things too, because my mind is like a big warren.

D But what comes out is very succinct.

C I hope so.

D Photography is unusual, in that it starts as monochrome and colour arrives later, which isn't how painting began. The palette of your work is very consistent, and quite restrained. Greys, blacks, browns, silvers.

C Palette is increasingly important to me, but it consists of found colour. I curated *Richard of York Gained Battle in Vain* at the Whitechapel Gallery in 2011, selecting 80 works from the Government Art Collection, works which had been exhibited in Downing Street or in far flung embassies. I hung the room as a colour spectrum which threw up all kinds of curious juxtapositions and political connotations. I loved that you could hang a Geeraerts painting next to a Peter Blake based on their hue. A few years later I curated a black-and-white room in the Royal Academy Summer Exhibition in 2014. The RA Show is usually an overwhelmingly cacophonous riot of colour, and I wanted to slow it all down and make something perhaps more politically considered, a bit more edgy.

With my recent photogravures I've tried using coloured inks, but they just don't work. The prints are of shadows, so they needed to be black and white. I'm thinking of using something called Space Ink, which is this pigment they're making out of pollution – basically capturing particles of dirt from the air. I like to make my own pigments. In fact, I've got a gun confiscated by the police which is being rusted into powder for me as we speak, which I'm going to use as a paint. I love all that particle stuff. I used to live in Shoreditch, not far from Clerkenwell, where there is an urban myth that the drains there are lined with silver because of all the photo lab chemicals that were poured down them. For my *Collected Death of Images* in 1996 I used the silver reclaimed from the photographic fixing process – a guy in his garage made sheets of accumulated silver residue for me. I like the idea in photography that to get a negative, you've got to remove the positive.

D It's interesting that when photography was new none of the talk was about what it lacked – they're not thinking, 'Oh, it's black and white, that's a problem.' They're thinking: 'That strangeness is part of its newness somehow.'

C This makes me think of that early black-and-white photograph of the Turin Shroud, how the negative image of it [taken by Secondia Pia in 1898] fleshed out the apparition, giving it a three-dimensional face. Suddenly it had become much more actualised – the image steals something from the object. It comes back to my polishing of the silver objects belonging to historical figures – the idea of stealing their thunder.

D There's also something about photography always being a kind of stealing. If it's not a stealing of souls then it's shadow-catching at least, or it's taking a surreptitious impression of something that maybe wasn't expecting it. And there's always something in your work that's hijacking something else and carrying it off.

C The most literal example of my hijacking is a site-specific piece I've made for the annual RA Summer Show. I photographed someone else's very popular bird etching; it was a large edition, which had garnered loads of red 'sold' spots, making me extremely covetous! I erased their image, leaving a blank piece of paper and the resplendent spots, then I editioned it and put it in the next summer exhibition, seemingly re-presenting last years' very popular 'monochrome'. At the end of the show when it had accrued its own spots, I re-photographed it *in situ*, an image within an image, and put it in the next annual show, etc. So over three consecutive years, *Stolen Thunder* became this running joke, a composition with red spots getting bigger and bigger. This year's exhibition features *Stolen Thunder (Twice Removed)* which is a redacted etching of a cat, so it appears as a black rectangle.

D I know you have talked about transubstantiation. The transformation of objects into images is such a kind of basic, fundamental, rudimentary thing, and yet the implications of it are so deep. I remember Duchamp describing how he wanted his ready-mades to strike his viewer with the force of a snapshot. And it's such an interesting idea – an object that's so familiar that you'd only see it as an image – it can have its effect right there.

C And you only need to see it for a nanosecond.

D You can contemplate it forever, but it can be taken away very quickly.

C I think I am interested in the unmade, rather than the ready-made. There is a photograph I have taken repeatedly – it's of the street map at Westminster Underground station, which is being scuffed by thousands of tourists pointing fingers. Now it looks like carnage.

D They destroy their own presence.

The Collected Death of Images 1996 (detail)
Silver reclaimed from photographic fix, 270 × 210 (approx.)

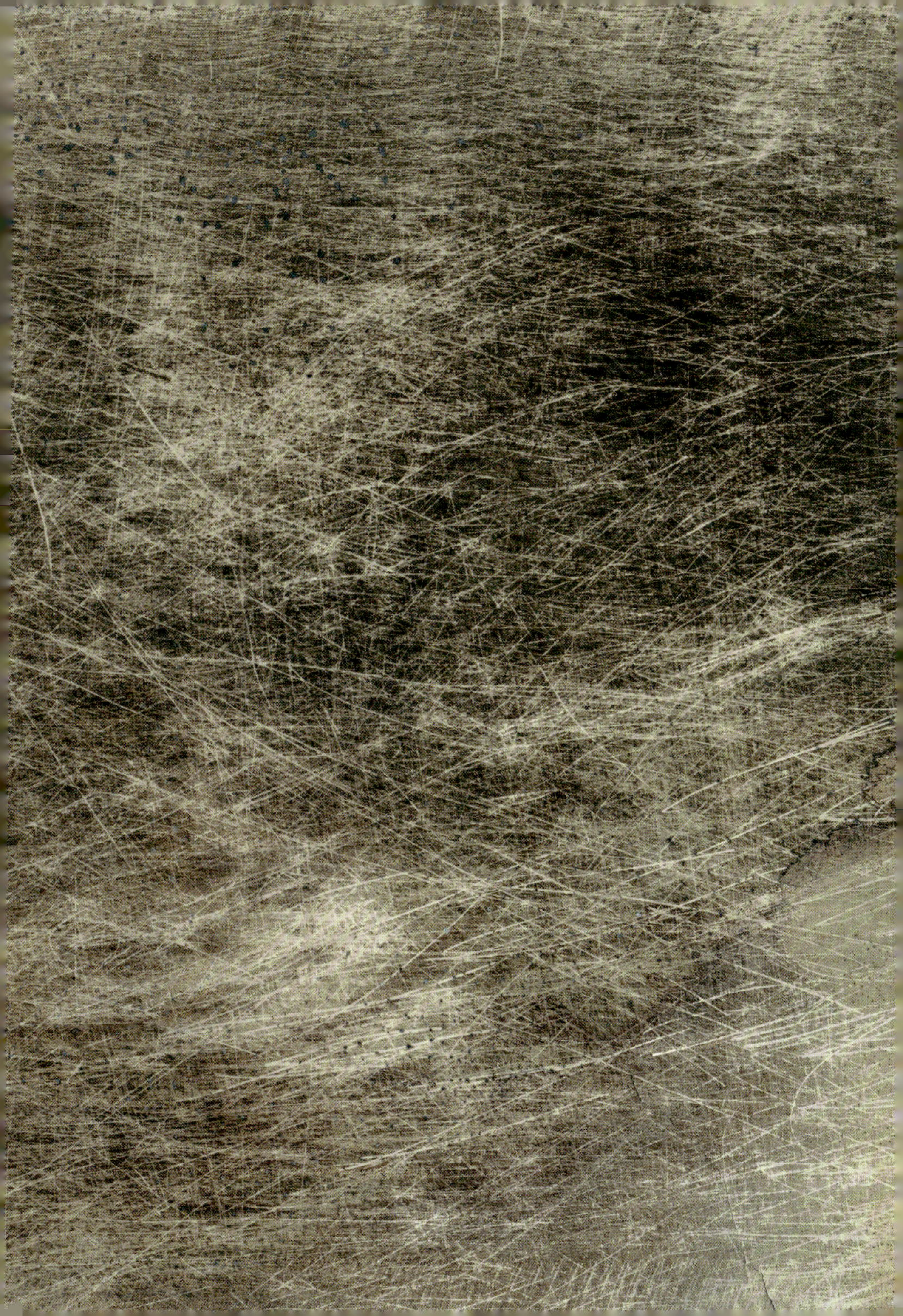

C I would pass by Pentonville prison quite often and noticed that the cracks in the prison wall had been repaired with filler, so they were reminiscent of abstract expressionist paintings. I recorded them on my phone in a series of images just before they disappeared entirely under a layer of magnolia paint (pp. 94–95). Later that day, amazingly, a convicted murderer escaped over the newly restored wall.

For *Avoided Object*, I was given permission by the Science Museum in London to use a camera that belonged to Rudolf Höss, who was the commandant of Auschwitz. They allowed me to take the camera out of storage to capture images of the clouds gathering above the museum. Using the camera to focus on such a benign subject was a way of undermining the horror of looking through the same lens as such an evil man. The infrared film I used gave the blameless clouds a feeling of foreboding (pp. 96–97).

D These works come back to your interest in the margins of things, the rebates, the backside, the ephemeral or invisible. It's like you're interested in the stage wings of life.

C As the saying goes, 'The back is as big as the front'.

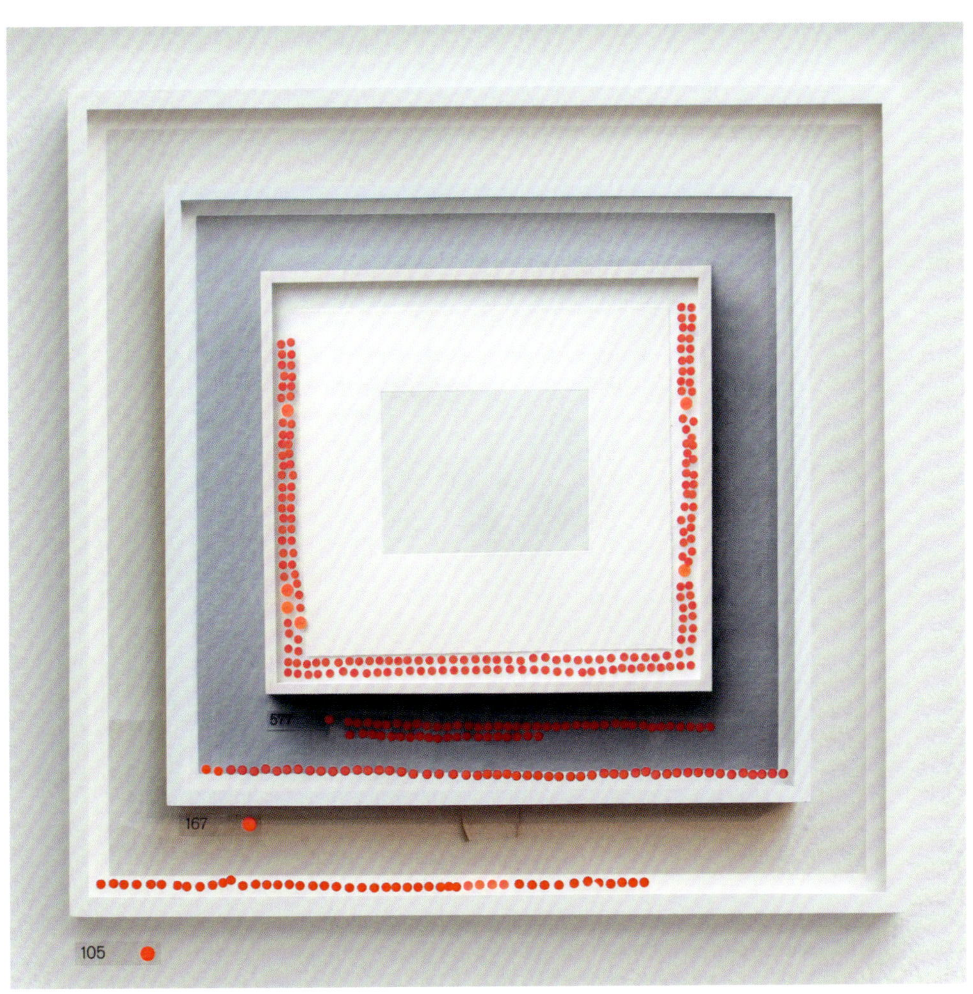

Stolen Thunder III 2015
Digital print on paper, 85.4 × 84.3

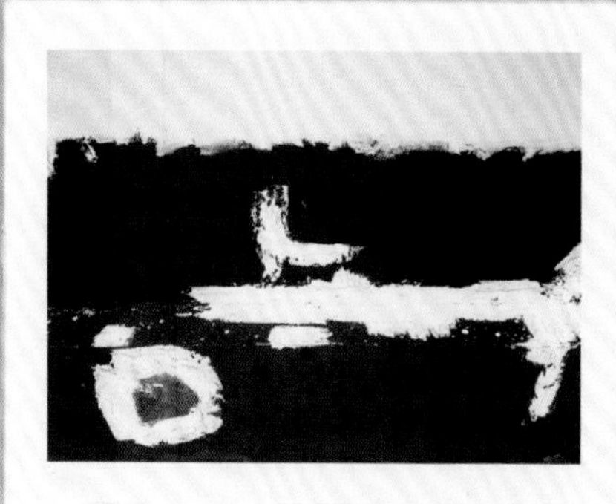
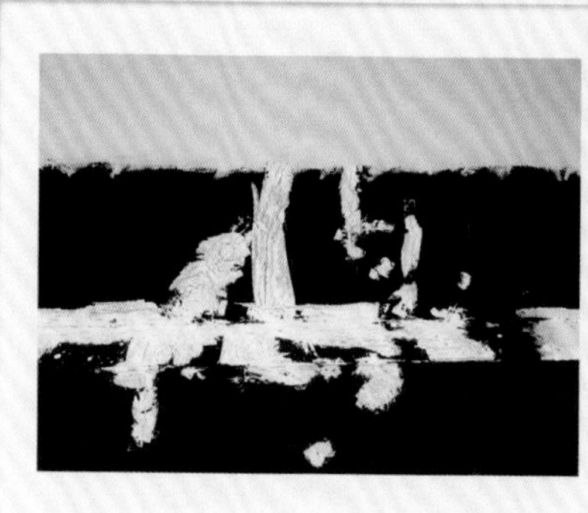
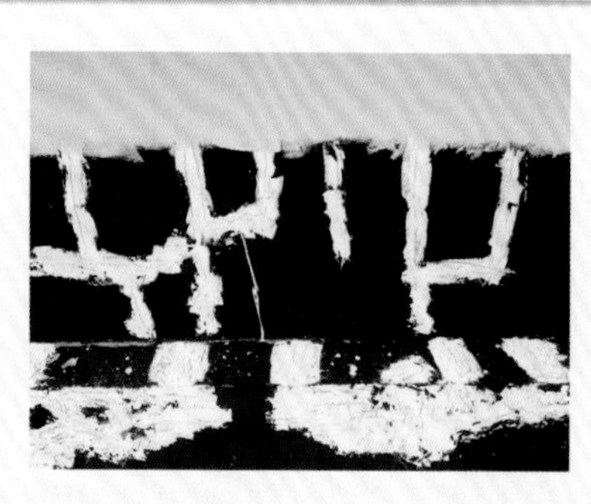
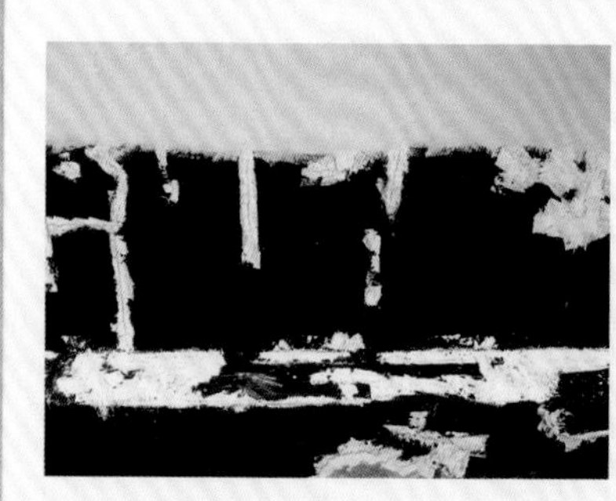
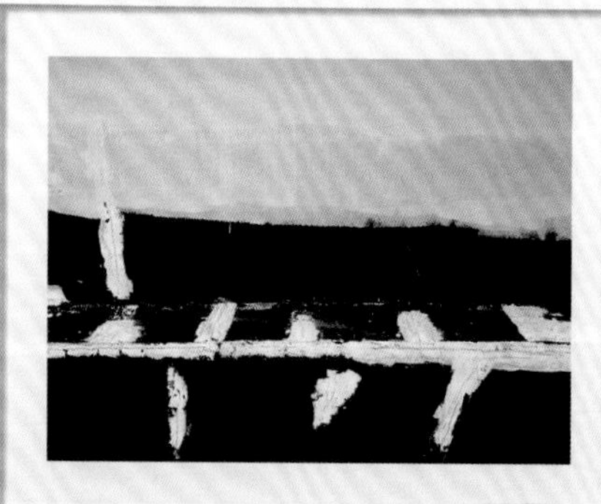
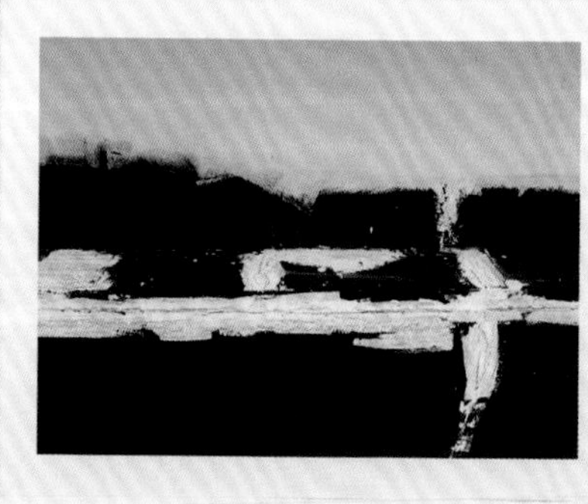

Prison Wall Abstract (A Man Escaped) 2012–13
Series of 12 digital prints on paper, each 60 × 76

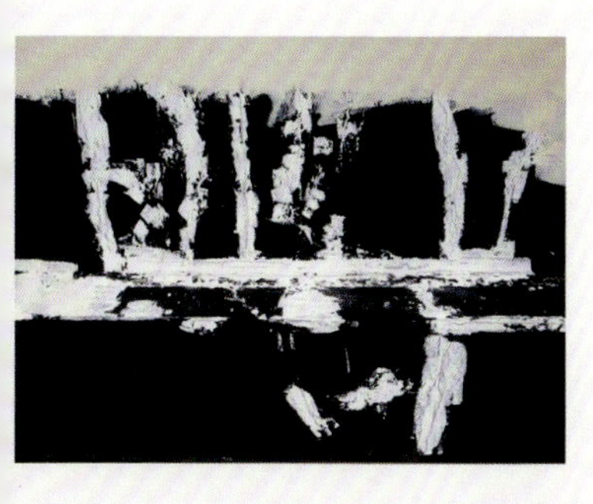
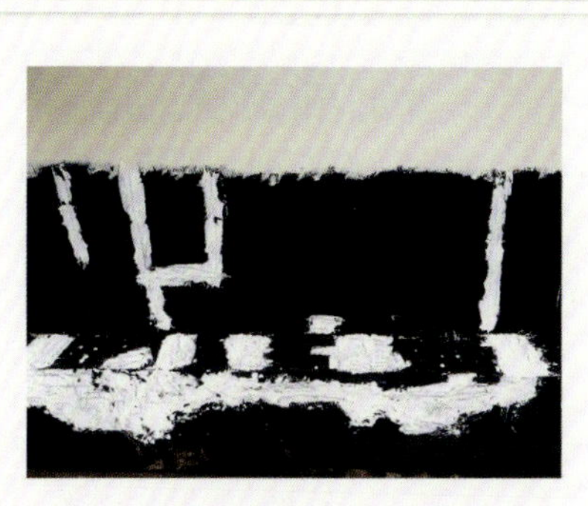
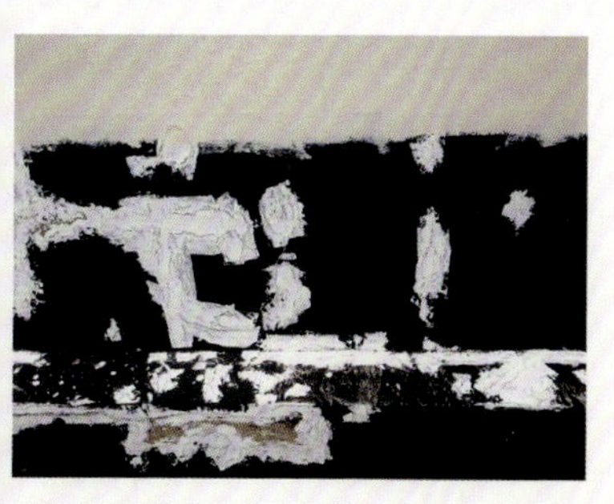
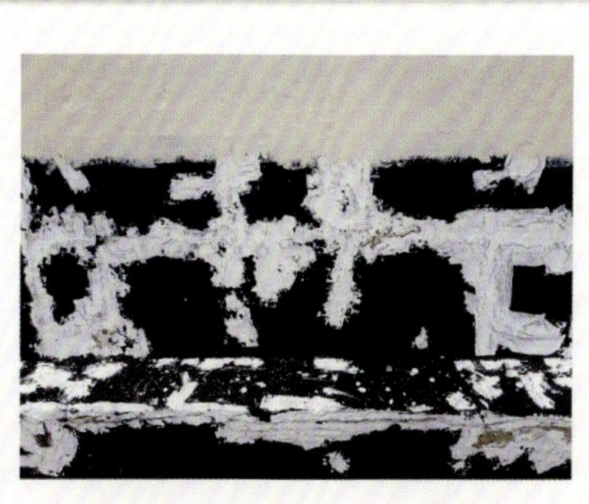
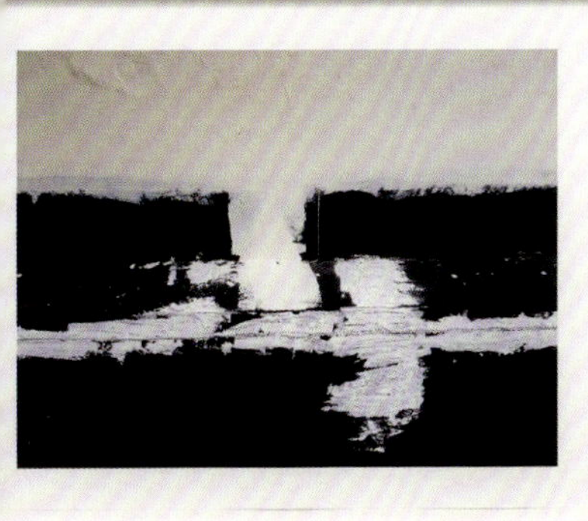
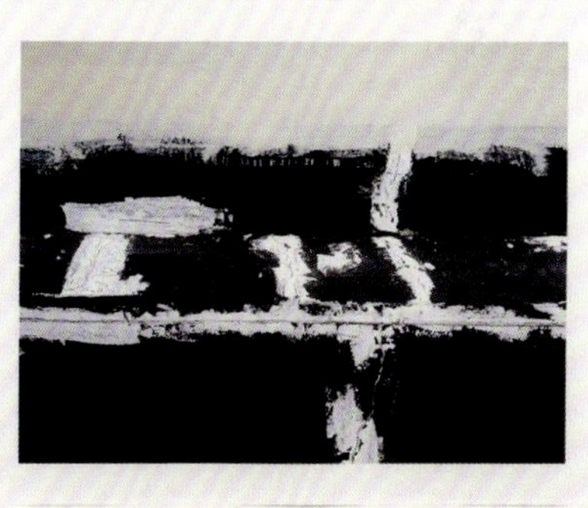

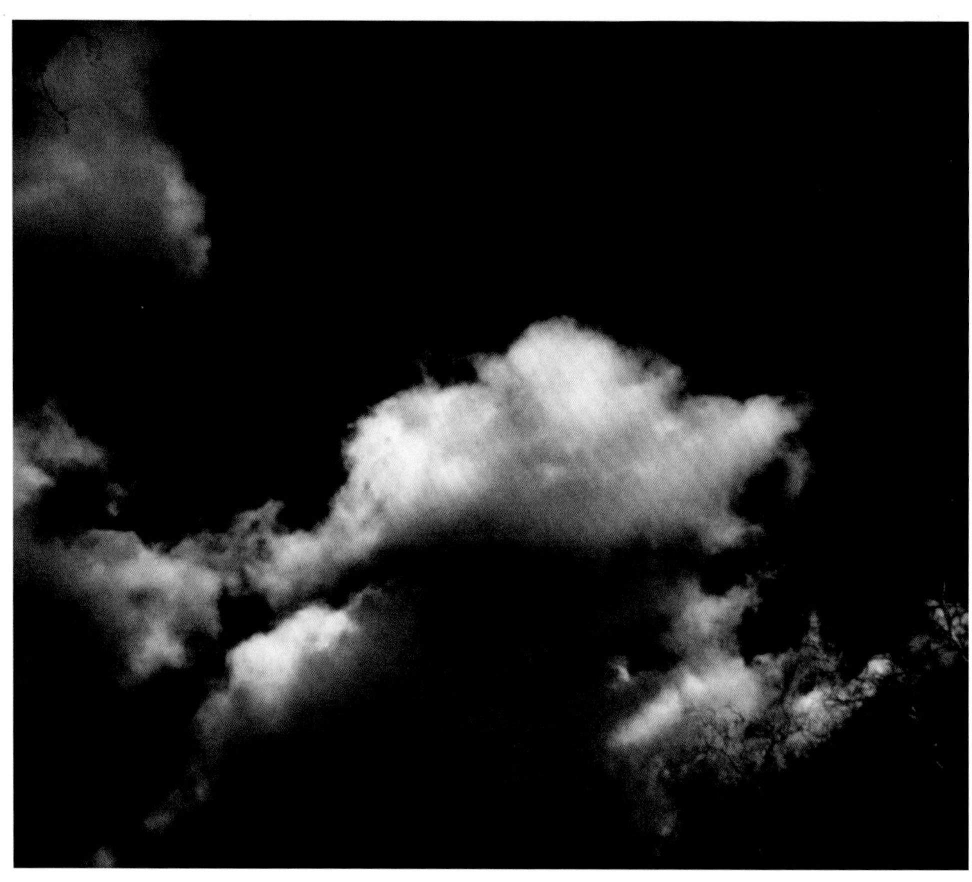

Avoided Object 1999
Infrared photographs of the sky above the Imperial War Museum, London, taken with a camera that belonged to Rudolf Höss, commandant of Auschwitz; each 62 × 62

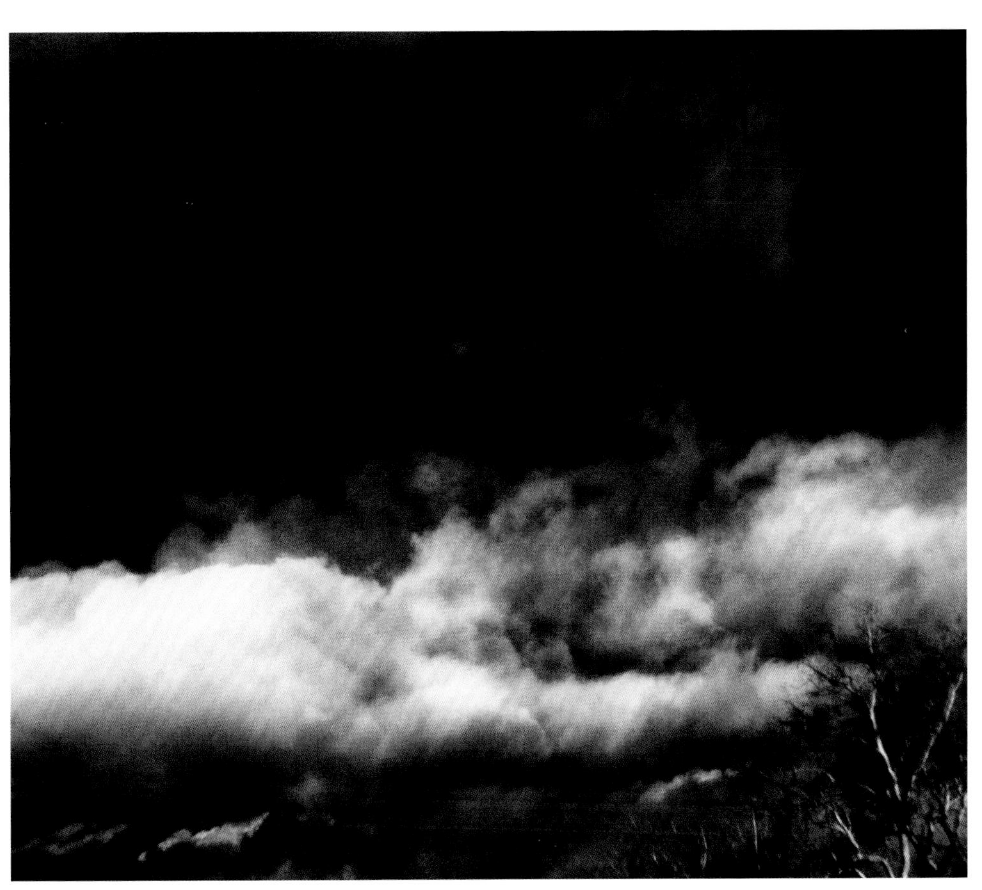

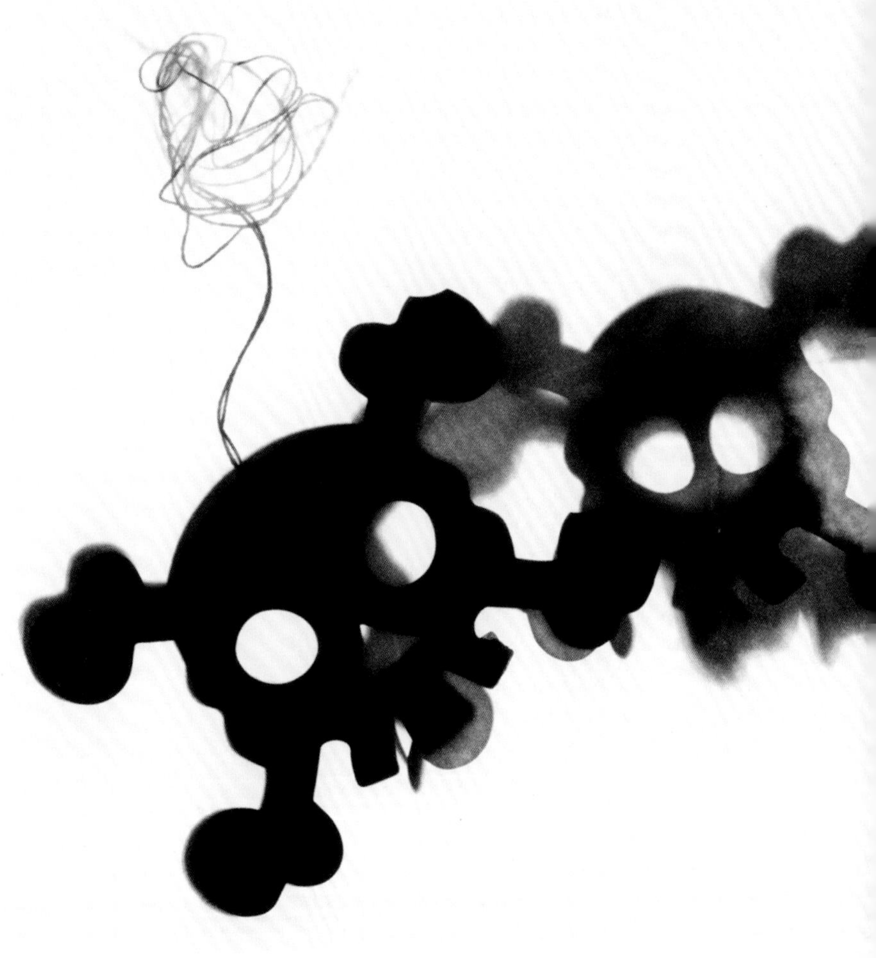

The End 2015
from **One Day This Glass Will Break**
Photogravure etching on paper, 55.7 × 80

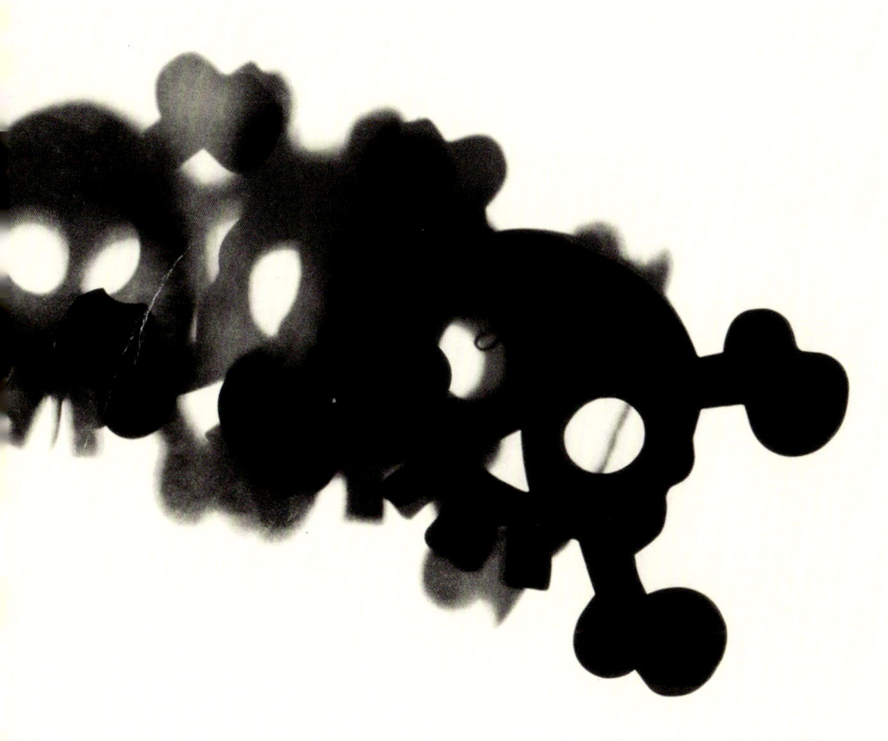

Published on the occasion of the Hayward Gallery Touring exhibition
Cornelia Parker: One Day This Glass Will Break

Exhibition curated by Antonia Shaw

Published in 2018 by
Hayward Gallery Publishing
Southbank Centre
Belvedere Road
London SE1 8XX, UK
www.southbankcentre.co.uk

Art Publisher: Rebecca Fortey
Sales Manager: Alex Glen
Project Manager, Publishing: Diana Adell
Catalogue designed by Herman Lelie
Layouts by Stefania Bonelli
Printed in Wales by Gomer Press

A catalogue record for this book is available from the British Library.

ISBN 978-1-85332-361-4

Distributed in North America, Central America and South America by
ARTBOOK | D.A.P.
75 Broad Street, Suite 630
New York, NY 10004
tel: +1 212 627 1999
www.artbook.com

Distributed in the UK and Europe by
Cornerhouse Publications
HOME, 2 Tony Wilson Place
Manchester, M15 4FN
tel: +44 (0)161 212 3466
www.cornerhousepublications.org

Picture credits

All images courtesy the artist with the following exceptions and clarifications:

Courtesy the artist and Alan Cristea Gallery, photo Peter White, FXP Photography, pp. 4, 25, 27, 29, 31, 33, 35, 37, 41, 47, 98–99
Courtesy the artist and Alan Cristea Gallery, pp. 76–77
Courtesy the artist, photo Edward Woodman: pp. 2, 52, 79
Courtesy the artist and Frith Street Gallery, photo courtesy the artist, p. 42, 94–95
Courtesy the artist and Frith Street Gallery, photo Edward Woodman, p. 78
Courtesy the artist and Ivory Press, pp. 81–82
Collection Caixa Foundation, photo Frank Kleinbach, pp. 84–85
With thanks to the Freud Museum, London, photo Edward Woodman, pp. 48–49
With thanks to the Freud Museum, London, courtesy the artist, p. 51
Collection Deutsche Bank, photo courtesy the artist, pp. 96–97
Collection Victoria and Albert Museum, photo courtesy the artist, pp. 96–97
Collection of the Metropolitan Museum of Art, New York, pp. 13, 15
Private collection, photo courtesy the artist, p. 44

Cover image: *The Collected Death of Images*, 1996 (detail), silver reclaimed from photographic fix, 270 × 210 (approx.)

Frontispiece: Process for *Thirty Pieces of Silver*: Cornelia Parker arranging silver plated objects, before they are crushed by a steamroller in 1988. The piece was first shown at the Ikon Gallery Birmingham 1988/89

p. 4
Articles of Glass, 2015, from *One Day This Glass Will Break*. Photogravure etching on paper, 79.7 × 56